THE
WHALE
WAR

DAVID DAY

THE WHALE WAR

SIERRA CLUB BOOKS   SAN FRANCISCO

Copyright© 1987 by David Day

Published simultaneously in Canada by Douglas & McIntyre Ltd., Vancouver, and in the United Kingdom by Routledge & Kegan Paul, London.

Cover photograph by Nakamura, Four by Five Inc.

Library of Congress Cataloging in Publication Data

Day, David, 1947–
   The whale war

   Includes index.
   1. Whales.   2. Whaling.   3. Wildlife conservation.
   4. International Whaling Commission – History.

I. Title.
QL737.C4D25 1987   639.9'795   87–4833
ISBN 0-87156-775-X
     0-87156-778-4 (pbk.)

     10   9   8   7   6   5   4   3   2   1

The moot point is, whether Leviathan can long endure so wide a chase, and so remorseless a havoc; whether he must not at last be exterminated from the waters, and the last whale, like the last man, smoke his last pipe, and then himself evaporate in the final puff.

HERMAN MELVILLE *Moby Dick*, 1851

CONTENTS

CONTENTS

FIGURES

ACKNOWLEDGMENTS

I would like to gratefully acknowledge the following individuals who specifically helped me in the preparation of this book at one stage or other over five years: Craig Van Note, Jean-Paul Fortom-Gouin, Paul Watson, Nick Carter, Campbell Plowden, Cleveland Amory, Christine Stevens, Bill Jordan, Rod Coronado, Stephan Ormrod, John May, Tina Harper, Lyle Watson, Lewis Registein, Cornellia Durrant, David McTaggert, Ray Gambol, Sidney Holt, Sir Peter Scott, Brian Davies, Charles Secrett, Sara Hambley, Jane McLernon, June Fenby, Richard Ellis, Jeremy Cherfais, Catherine Caufield, Patricia Forkan, Bob Hunter, Ian Macphail, Remi Parimentier, Tom Garrett, John Frizell, Katherine Kay-Mouat, Elke Stenzel, David Garrick, Linda Rogers, David McColl, Paul Vodden, Alan Macnow, I. V. Nikonorov, Kunio Yonezawa.

In addition I would like to thank the following organizations: Monitor, International Whaling Commission, Greenpeace, Sea Shepherd, Animal Welfare Institute, Fund for Animals, Humane Society of America, People's Trust for Endangered Species, Royal Society for Prevention of Cruelty to Animals, Earth Trust, Cetacean Society, Friends of the Earth, International Fund for Animal Welfare, Center for Environmental Education, Environmental Investigation Agency, Japanese Whaling Association.

Also a special thanks to Terry Jones, Margaret Atwood, Al Purdy, Allan Thornton, Kathryn Court and the Canada Council.

PROLOGUE

OF WHALES AND MEN

They say the sea is cold, but the sea contains the hottest blood of all, and the wildest, the most urgent.

D. H. LAWRENCE *Whales Weep Not*

The heart of the blue whale is the height of a tall man and weighs half a ton. It beats like a huge kettle drum and its valves pump a sea of hot blood along the whale's 100 foot, 160-ton bulk, through arteries so big a child could crawl through them.

The whale is at the heart of a guerilla war of resistance that has spread over all the world: it is the symbol of the ecology movement and emblematic of the fate of all species on the planet. The battle line has been drawn here. If this amazing animal, the largest ever to exist on the planet, cannot be saved from the ruthless exploitation of a handful of men, what chance of survival have other species? Around the banner of the movement to save the whale have gathered ecologists, scientists, educators, professional activists, entertainers, schoolchildren and people from every profession, political persuasion and race.

Against them stand the men who hunt the whale. They are few, but they are men of influence. Some are men like the late Aristotle Onassis who in his pursuit of a fortune in the whaling industry in the 1950s violated every conceivable regulation and international law relating to whales. He recognized no closed season, no national territorial waters, no protected species, no minimum length requirement and no ban on hunting nursing mothers or even suckling young. A man so ostentatious and proud of his destruction of the whale that the bar in his private yacht, the *Christina*, was fitted throughout with whale ivory and polished bone and – as a kind of visual joke in the most appalling taste – sported bar stools made from the penises of sperm whales.

Other whalers are less flamboyant; most are simply diligent, hard-working men. Not bad or evil, but just determined and refusing in the face of everything to see or believe what the consequences of their actions are. Such men in other times have brought about the extinction of the passenger pigeon, the great auk, the blue buck, the Steller sea cow, the Caribbean monk seal, the Bali tiger and hundreds of others. Such men push species after species into the oblivion of extinction and call it honest industry: a work ethic that would stop the heart of all life on the planet if some means might be found to profit by it.

I remember very well from the moment that I fell from the boat and felt my feet strike some soft substance. I looked up and saw a big-ribbed canopy of light pink and white descending over me, and the next moment I felt myself drawn downward, feet first, and I realised that I was being swallowed by a whale. I was drawn lower and lower; a wall of flesh surrounded me and hemmed me in on every side, yet the pressure was not painful and the flesh easily gave way like soft india-rubber before my slightest movement.

Suddenly I found myself in a sack much larger than my body, but completely dark. I felt about me; and my hands came in contact with several fishes, some of which seemed to be still alive, for they squirmed in my fingers, and slipped back to my feet. Soon I felt a great pain in my head and my breathing became more and more difficult. At the same time I felt a terrible heat; it seemed to consume me, growing hotter and hotter. My eyes became coals of fire in my head, and I believed every moment that I was condemned to perish in the belly of a whale. It tormented me beyond all endurance, while at the same time the awful silence of the terrible prison weighed me down. I tried to rise, to move my arms and legs, to cry out. All action was now impossible, but my brain seemed abnormally clear; and with a full comprehension of my awful fate, I finally lost all consciousness.

This fascinating narrative was written by 35-year-old James Bartley, an English sailor on the *Star of the East*, who on 25 August 1891, while whaling in the South Atlantic off the Falkland Islands, was reportedly swallowed by a whale. What is so extraordinary is not so much that Bartley was swallowed by an enraged sperm whale in the midst of the hunt – there have been a few other such reports – but that he lived to tell the story.

According to this widely published account of the incident, within a couple of hours of the whale's swallowing Bartley, it was killed and brought to the mother ship. There, after hours of butchering, the stomach section was opened and the astonished crewmen found the lost Bartley: unconscious, bleached to a deathly white by the gastric acids, but still living. For two weeks Bartley remained in a near delirious condition, but apart from his almost albino state (which remained with him all his life), he made a full recovery.

Where whales are concerned, mythical incidents and tall tales are legion, and most contemporary scientists do not believe Bartley could possibly survive more than a very few minutes in a whale's belly.

It is difficult to be entirely dismissive about anything concerning whales – they are a constant source of the miraculous. Fabrication or not, Bartley's narrative is a remarkable and not inaccurate description of what the experience might be like. But Bartley's tale is, of course, a universal story updated. On the wall of my study, as I write this book, hangs a Kwakiutl Indian totem sculpture of a whale with a man in its belly. It is a variation on the story of Jonah, and further variations are told over and over by virtually every culture that knows of the existence of the whale.

There are many legends of the whale that have proved to be true, and there are a large number of fishy tales that are totally false, that in the end perhaps tell us far more about humans than about whales. However, the beast itself needs no exaggeration to amaze us. The facts are quite enough.

The whale is a wondrous life form, not just because of its size but also because of the unbelievable speed of its growth. Measuring its growth from the ovum at conception, through eleven months of gestation, until it reaches one year of age and 26 tons, the blue whale is the fastest growing organism – either plant or animal – on earth.

As any enthusiast will tell you, whales are the Grand Canyon and the Mount Everest of the animal world. The blue whale weighs as much as 2,000 men. The brain of the sperm whale, at 20lbs, is six times the size of the human brain. The bowhead whale has a mouth as wide as an interstate ferry ramp, which would allow two semi-trailer trucks to enter side by side. The humpback whale sings arias that can be heard over a thousand miles of open ocean. The grey whale has a 7,000-miles migration pattern – the longest of any mammal on earth ranging from the Arctic waters of Alaska and Siberia to the Baja Gulf in Mexico. The killer whale propels itself beyond the explanation of science at speeds of 40 miles per hour and is the fastest animal in the sea.

With the whales we seem to enter the realm of an ancient and long vanished world, or a fairy-tale world that never was. But the time is now, and the living whale is a reality that dwarfs the dinosaurs of prehistoric times and even the mythical giants and dragons of our imagination.

My first close encounter with whales was in the summer of 1959, when I was nearly 12. As a child living on the southern tip of Vancouver Island on Canada's west coast, I often sighted from the shore schools of killer whales and, on occasion, larger great whales. But that summer I had an unasked-for closer look.

My father and I were salmon fishing from our boat just a short distance from the shore when suddenly two killer whales like inflatable rubber submarines emerged on either side of our boat. Their slick black backs and high dorsal fins simply rose up huge out of the deep green waters. The whales were so close that the misty spray from the blow hole of one whale lightly spattered across my face, and I remember thinking, without actually daring to do so, that I could almost reach out and touch its back. Their appearance was so unexpected that I simply sat with a child's wide-eyed fascination, staring at them. My father, on the other hand, quickly leapt up without a word, grasped the wheel and, without stopping to even pull in the fishing lines, opened the engine full throttle. We bolted suddenly from between the two whales, then turned the wheel sharply and fled for the safety of the harbour.

My father, like most others who fished on the coast, had heard lurid tales of boats overturned or rammed, and of fishermen knocked overboard by the killer whales. Their killing of larger whales as they hunted in packs like wolves of the sea, tearing the tongues and lips from their huge prey, suggested to many that although no one had heard first-hand of anybody being eaten by a killer whale, if you fell in the water around one, the whale would display much the same discretion as a great white shark.

It seems strange now to tell how we fled from a couple of curious adolescent killer whales, who playfully popped up simply to take a closer look at us. Today in these waters nobody would run from the whales. In fact, tourists pay guides good money to track them down just so they can catch a glimpse and take a picture. In nearby aquariums people are having killer whales perform tricks. People ride on their backs and even dare to put their heads in the 'killers'' toothy mouths.

But until the mid-1960s, knowledge of the killer whale (and most other whales, for that matter) was based largely on rumour and conjecture. Most took the term killer whale literally, and assumed the beast had a brutal nature and vicious habits. You would find few who saw any good in the killer whale. Fishermen and sportsmen, if they carried rifles aboard their boats, would randomly shoot passing killer whales out of hand. In the 1950s *Time Magazine* was able to print, without disapproval or concern:

> Killer whales. Savage sea cannibals up to 30 feet long with teeth like bayonets . . . the Icelandic government appealed to the U.S., which has thousands of men stationed at a lonely NATO airbase on the subarctic island. Seventy-nine bored GIs responded with enthusiasm. Armed with rifles and machine guns, one posse of Americans climbed into four small boats and in one morning wiped out a pack of 100 killers. . . .
>
> First the killers were rounded up into a tight formation with concentrated machine gun fire, then moved out again one by one, for the final blast which would kill them. . . . As one was wounded, the others would set upon it and tear it to pieces with their jagged teeth.

Today, most people would be appalled at such a massacre. And in fact, by US law, such an incident – either military or civilian – would now certainly result in prosecution. Also, even school-children these days would point out that the writer had entirely fabricated the killing-frenzy episode at the end of the article.

Killer whales emphatically do not cannibalize one another like sharks when wounded or killed. Yet when the article was printed, *Time* did not receive even one dissenting letter.

This attitude remained prevalent until 1964. In that year, while the US Air Force was still using killer whales as practice targets for live machine-gun strafing runs in the North Atlantic, the first killer whale ever to be captured alive was taken off Vancouver Island. This animal, called Moby Doll, had been shot and harpooned, but it survived three months in captivity. The following year, another killer whale, called Namu, was taken in nearby waters and survived captivity for one year.

These captive whales, and the few score that followed them, overnight changed people's attitude towards the species. Reluctant ambassadors though they were, the whales' gentle and friendly behaviour, obvious intelligence and playful nature totally charmed the public. It was soon clear that killer whales were not brutal, shark-like predators at all. With their striking black and white markings, they became cheerful and popular 'pandas of the sea' in the public mind. Within a couple of years, it was difficult to find anyone at all familiar with them who had the least fear of the once notorious 'killer' whale. Indeed, the name was used less and less, and its proper scientific name, Orca, came into common use.

This rapid shift of public attitude towards the killer whale from antipathy in the early 1960s to total sympathy by 1970 coincided with the same period of radical change in attitude towards all the great whales. Opinion moved from indifference during what was the most wanton destruction of the whale in history (some 60,000 a year in the 1960s), to shock and alarm by the early 1970s, when some nations continued to hunt despite the obvious collapse of all whale populations.

All but a handful of nations now viewed whaling not just with disapproval but as completely unjustified economically and morally. It was seen not so much as an 'industry' as a programme of extermination. In 1972 the United Nations Conference on the Human Environment was held in Stockholm, and in a clear expression of a wide popular belief in the right of whales to survival, there was a vote of 52 nations to 0 in favour of an immediate cessation of all commercial whaling.

Yet after that vote the killing went on, and though diminished, it still goes on today. The 1972 United Nations vote proved not to be the end of whaling but rather the real starting point – the declaration – of the Whale War. The battle of save the whale began then in earnest. It has been a bitter and hard fight, and it is a conflict that has spread to every corner of the globe.

PART ONE

The campaign to save whales is a rare and refreshing example of intelligence in the service of something other than self-interest.

GEORGE F. WILL   Washington Post

1

THE FRONT LINE

1 THE ECO-GUERILLAS

The high steel prow of the *Vlastny*, the 150-foot Russian hunter-killer whaler, is plunging through the rough Pacific swell. At the end of the catwalk that stretches from the bridge to the prow is mounted a 90-mm cannon loaded with a 160-lb exploding grenade harpoon with foot-long barbed hooks. Surging with the swells in a high speed chase, the gunner hunches over the cannon with deadly concentration.

Behind the *Vlastny*, at some distance, is the massive hulk of the 10-story high, 750-foot *Dalniy Vostok* (literally 'Far East'). It is the mother-ship, the floating factory that is fed by the *Vlastny* and a fleet of five other harpoon boats.

Before the *Vlastny*'s gunner is the object of his pursuit: a dozen sperm whales, their sleek backs rising out of the water. The whales have been chased to exhaustion by the powerful diesel engines of the hunter-killer vessel, and the *Vlastny* is now closing in for the kill.

But there is a bizarre and entirely unprecedented element in this particular hunt. Between the gunner and the whales are three of those small, inflatable commando speedboats known as Zodiacs. Each Zodiac holds two self-confessed ecology guerillas, would-be protectors of the whale. Like pacifists who lie down in the path of oncoming tanks, these eco-guerillas place a human barrier between the gun and the whale. They are gambling that a concern for the loss of human lives will save the whales, where concern for the survival of the species itself has failed.

They gamble with an unrepentant foe. The *Vlastny* gunner fires his cannon, and the harpoon hurtles almost directly over the centre Zodiac as it dips in the trough of an ocean swell. The shot is made with deadly accuracy: it strikes the back of a whale. There is an explosion of spray and foam, a whirlpool of boiling blood. The steel harpoon cable comes down, slicing the water like a guillotine, barely an arm's length from the wildly veering Zodiac.

That was 27 June 1975, and it was the first ever gladiatorial between whalers and ecologists on the open seas. The eco-guerillas were from the then-obscure Canadian direct-action ecology group called Greenpeace. It was a brave – and some believed foolish – effort, and although it did not save that particular whale, it had a great deal to do with saving many others.

Fortunately, the Greenpeacers had equipped one of their Zodiacs with a cameraman, who, almost as much by sheer good luck as skill, managed to capture the most critical moment of the encounter on film. It was then broadcast in America by Walter Cronkite's CBS TV News, and on virtually every other major television network in the western world. For the first time the Save the Whale movement was front page news, and for many people it was the first they were to know of the Whale War. For the first time the vague rumours of this ecology war at sea were crystallized in vivid images, and the impact was startling.

Robert Hunter, Greenpeace's director at that time (and one of the two Zodiac riders who had the Russian harpoon hurtle over their heads), was himself a classic sixties long-haired and bearded 'gonzo' journalist, and he knew the importance of the dramatic image in popular media. He later wrote a perceptive comment on the significance of the event and how it had changed the image of whaling in the popular imagination:

> Instead of small boats and giant whales, giant boats and small whales; instead of courage killing whales, courage saving whales; David had become Goliath, Goliath was now David; if the mythology of Moby Dick and Captain Ahab had dominated human consciousness about Leviathan for over a century, a whole new age was in the making.

The degree to which the Ahab and Moby Dick story reversed itself became amusingly evident some time later when American television viewers were confronted by none other than Gregory Peck, the actor who portrayed Ahab in the film version of *Moby Dick*, in a television advertisement sponsored by the Animal Welfare Institute.

Peck let his views on whaling be known in no uncertain terms:

A hundred years ago during whaling's romantic heyday, a three-year expedition netted an average of thirty-seven whales. Today a modern Japanese or Russian whaling fleet can eliminate thirty-seven whales a day with brutal military precision. There are cheap, plentiful substitutes for all whale products. Unfortunately, there are no substitutes for whales.

Evidently Captain Ahab was on the side of the whales these days.

Robert Hunter later observed about that first high-seas showdown: 'We were faced with knowing that the next time we set out to block a harpoon shot, there would be no kidding ourselves that the Russians were unwilling to take a chance on killing us. We would have to crank ourselves up that much more.'

And crank themselves up they did.

2 THE RUSSIAN FRONT

Greenpeace began in 1970 as a rather ragtag local ecology group, but its dramatically combative pacifism in such events as the whale campaign suddenly hurled it into the public mind as the password for ecological activism, and its influence mushroomed overnight. In 1976 and 1977 Greenpeace escalated the Whale War on the Russian front. Targeting the Russian armada in the Pacific whaling grounds, forced five more extended confrontations on the high seas. Also, it rapidly increased its armament. It acquired the *James Bay*, a big, fast ex-minesweeper – or as the Greenpeace crew insisted on calling it, a 'mindsweeper'.

In mid-July 1976 Greenpeace was again tracking down the huge factory ship the *Dalniy Vostok*, and its killer fleet. This time Greenpeace found the *Vostok* hunting midway between California and Hawaii. Fearing the worst, the eco-guerillas ran their three Zodiacs between the whales and the harpoon guns. But this time the gunners did not shoot. Instead, the harpoon boats retired, and the whales fled to freedom. The human barrier tactics had at last worked! The *Vostok* and her fleet steamed away, in an attempt to leave the Greenpeace ship behind. The *James Bay* pursued, driving the whalers further and further from the whaling grounds. Greenpeace kept up the chase for two days and nights before lack of fuel forced it to turn back to port in Hawaii.

The Greenpeacers were in a celebratory mood, for they felt their blockade had pushed the Russians into retreat. It was obvious, though, that a decision had been made in advance; the Russians did not wish to repeat the publicity of the year before, for they frankly feared another incident might trigger a trade embargo that had been threatened in 1974 for previous Russian whaling violations. Whatever the reason, they retreated. The *James Bay* resupplied and refuelled then made that year's second run at the by now totally harassed *Vostok* some 1,300 miles off Hawaii.

It was a repeat performance of the previous encounter by the human barrier Zodiac patrol: the harpoon boats withdrew, the *Vostok* fleet retreated and the Greenpeacers pursued it north-wards until low fuel once more forced them to turn back.

The following year, at the end of July 1977, Greenpeace again had the *James Bay* in action on the Russian front. This time it hunted down the Russians' second whaling fleet the *Vladivostok* – the huge sister ship of the *Vostok* – and her eight killer boats, just 700 miles off the California coast. As on previous encounters the ecologists were able to film the whale killings and document the taking of undersized whales. However, the *Vladivostok* suddenly became impatient with the fast-manoeuvring Zodiacs, and a harpoon was fired with almost fatal results over two Greenpeace commandos.

A few weeks later a second ship joined Greenpeace's eco-navy. This was the even larger *Ohana Kai*, a swift-running former sub-chaser run by the newly formed Greenpeace-Hawaii. The *Ohana Kai* hunted down the first Russian whaling fleet about 1,000 miles north of Hawaii. Since the *Vostok* could not outrun the sub-chaser, she kept up a long, slow retreat, resulting in an extremely costly fuel bill for her fleet. Furthermore, the *Vostok* hunted no whales while the ecologists shadowed her. After a week in pursuit, a team of Greenpeacers boarded the *Vostok* and distributed anti-whaling propaganda to the crew.

Late in August the *James Bay* was making Greenpeace's third run of the summer at the Russians. It was the *Vladivostok* fleet again, but she too had been tamed by the earlier encounter, for while she was followed by the Canadian Greenpeacers for a week, she remained dormant. And the *Vladivostok* too submitted to a Greenpeace boarding.

By the end of 1977, although the whaling nations were unrepentant in their whaling policies, the tide of public opinion was massively against them. This was not due to Greenpeace; however its activities were the most dramatic manifestation of a popular sentiment, and for the first time activists were attempting to physically act upon that impulse. It gave the public heart to fight harder. International press coverage – provoked by the eco-guerilla confrontations – combined with lobbying by conservation-minded governments and scores of environmental organizations were placing unheard of pressure on the whaling nations.

And major changes did indeed come. It was hotly debated whether this was because of international pressure or economic necessity caused by the destruction of whale stocks. However, 1977 saw the world's remaining pelagic (deep sea) factory ship fleets reduced from *five* (two Russian and three Japanese) to only *two*: one each for Russia and Japan. Whatever the cause of the change, for the Save the Whale forces it was a victory.

3 SOUTH PACIFIC

The worst years of whale slaughtering in the South Pacific were in the 1930s. During that decade the whaling stations of Australia and New Zealand obliterated the last great migratory herds of humpback whales. The humpbacks are the 'singing whales', the leapers who are distinguished by their great 'wings' or pectoral fins that allow them to be, as one early ship's captain described, 'as graceful as swallows on the wing'.

The slaughter of the humpback herds was not only conducted on a large scale, it was also practised by many in an indescribably cruel manner. In well-documented reports there are descriptions of how the whales were hunted by fast motor launches mounted with light harpoon guns. The guns and harpoons were not intended to kill the whale, but merely to secure it so that a hollow spear connected to an air compressor could be inserted into the whale's body. Then, in one of the most painful means of killing conceivable, the whale was inflated with air *while still alive.*

This was the standard procedure at some stations. It saved the whalers the loss of those whales that sank upon death. Much better to inflate them before death than after, and this left much less damage than explosive harpoons. If the tortured animal struggled on too long, a long lance with a cast iron head loaded with a pound and a half of gelignite was inserted into its thorax and electrically ignited. Death soon followed.

Perhaps, then, the 40-foot long white vinyl inflatable whale pumped up and launched in a lake next to the hotel that housed the 1977 International Whaling Commission conference in Canberra, Australia, was a kind of black joke, a reminder of this horrible method of slaughter in the South Pacific. Whatever the point, the white whale – nicknamed Willie the Whale – was swept up and ceremoniously carried to a park directly across the street from the IWC meetings and served as a centrepiece for the Save the Whale demonstrators for several days.

Then came the day of vengeance for the inflatable whale, as Willie the Whale made his presence felt rather forcefully to the Japanese delegation who until this point had done their very best to ignore him. On the fourth day of the convention, the Japanese delegates found the corridor to their conference room entirely filled by Willie's bulk. Police and hotel staff were dutifully obliged on behalf of their Japanese guests – in the full glare of television news camera lights – to harpoon and butcher the hapless whale with kitchen carving knives in order to reclaim the room for the delegation.

On the final day of the conference, the ghost of Willie made one last appearance. The deflated remains were placed in a giant coffin, and he was brought back to the park where taps was played on a trumpet to mourn his cruel slaughter. There was a moment of silence. Then a proclamation that his death would not be in vain, that his spirit would prevail.

So as battles raged in the summer of 1977 on the Russian front of the North Pacific with the Greenpeace eco-navy, down in the

South Pacific another front had opened. Australia was the last English-language nation in the world to maintain a commercial whaling industry, and now it was coming under pressure to end its venture. Many environmental groups over several years had attempted to make an issue out of Western Australia's sole whaling station, the Cheynes Beach Whaling Company, a shore station that had a spotter plane and three hunter-killer boats in King George Sound. Probably the most effective and established of these groups was Project Jonah, which had strong support in Australia and pursued a policy of public education and political lobbying as a key to ending whaling.

As news of Greenpeace's encounters was coming in from the Russian front, another group employing Greenpeace's direct action tactics was also investing in Zodiacs. With token Greenpeace support, this was the Whale and Dolphin Coalition, set up by Jean-Paul Fortom-Gouin, a Bahamas-based Frenchman. A talented investment analyst when he is not an environmental activist or diplomatic mole (he managed to surface as the Panamanian Commissioner to the IWC!), Fortom-Gouin has for years been a mainstay of many Save the Whale campaigns. It seems strange that this likeable and mercurial Frenchman, himself physically small, should become so obsessed with the saving of the planet's largest animals. Whatever his reasons – for no material gain whatever – Fortom-Gouin has put considerable resources into the movement. Indeed it was he who largely financed Greenpeace-Hawaii's Russian expedition. And, it was rumoured, he was the 'French connection' behind the Willie the Whale episode.

It was against the Cheynes Beach Whaling Company that environmentalists launched their attack. Like the Greenpeacers before them, they raced the hunters out to the whaling grounds and tried to place themselves in the line of fire. It was an extended campaign, and during September they were brought to near-fatal encounters when the Australian whalers twice fired harpoons over them. Once, with Fortom-Gouin in the Zodiac that stood between the gun and the whales, the shot had come so close that the harpoon line caught the propellor of the Zodiac's engine and lifted it out of the water, nearly flipping the eco-guerillas into the shark-infested waters some 40 miles off the Australian coast.

4 THE CHILDREN'S CRUSADE

Sorting through recent literature and photographs of whaling still going on in the world today, I find a picture of a blond boy playing on a beach on the Faroes Islands where fishermen are cutting up and slaughtering pilot whales. The almost angelic face of the boy is intently concentrated in his play. He has found a toy and is having difficulty dragging it up the shingle beach, and tugs severely on the rope he has attached to it. The toy is the pure white foetus of a pilot whale that has been torn from the belly of its slaughtered mother.

It makes me think of an older picture of a full-grown man, smiling proudly with his head just visible over the back of a 25-foot blue whale foetus that he and his fellow workers have just cut out of the huge mother whale with their long flensing razors. Such men breed such children. The brutality is a kind of contagion.

But the reverse can also be true. The innocence of childhood can remain uncorrupted and sensitive to the world. And if ever there was a case for a children's crusade of innocence coming to a good cause and persuading the world to it, perhaps Australia's South Pacific Whale War is as fine an example as any.

Useful as the direct action tactics in Australia may have been in drawing the attention of the public to the whaling issue, in the end it was the broad non-confrontational tactics of the quieter, or at least more diplomatically acceptable, groups that turned the tide in Australia.

By the summer of 1977, some 70 per cent of the Australian public was against whaling. Through public education programmes such as Project Jonah, through domestic political pressure and international censure, Australian whaling became less and less appealing to those in government.

Finally, as several Australian newspapers were later to point out, it was perhaps the most vivid example of hope for the future lying in the hands of children. For among Project Jonah and other Save the Whale group converts was 11-year-old Phoebe Fraser, the daughter of the Prime Minister Malcolm Fraser.

Throughout her father's election campaign in 1977, she wore a Save the Whale badge, and during that campaign Fraser told representatives from Project Jonah that he was 'coming under pressure from home to stop the killing of whales'. Consequently, immediately after his successful election, Prime Minister Fraser appointed an independent inquiry into Australian whaling policy led by the former Chief Justice of Papua New Guinea, Sir Sydney Frost.

By December 1978 the results of the inquiry were in and soon after its recommendations were adopted by the government in a most dramatic turnabout. When Fraser announced the following April the official adoption of the report, not only was whaling outlawed in Australia and banned within the 200-miles limit of its waters, the country now took the stance that it was opposed to whaling worldwide on both scientific and *ethical* grounds. Fraser said: 'The harpooning of these animals is offensive to many people who regard killing these special and intelligent animals as inconsistent with the ideals of mankind, and without any valid economic purpose in mitigation.'

The official government statement put it plainly:

> Australia should pursue a policy of opposition to whaling and this policy should be pursued both domestically and inter-nationally through the IWC and other organizations. . . . Satisfactory substitutes are already available for nearly all whale products. Therefore the importation into Australia of all whale products and goods containing them are to be banned.

From its position as a whaling nation, Australia, in one of the most complete turnabouts in conservationist history, became a fervent anti-whaling nation. It had stated that *whaling was morally wrong* – and it was the first nation to do so.

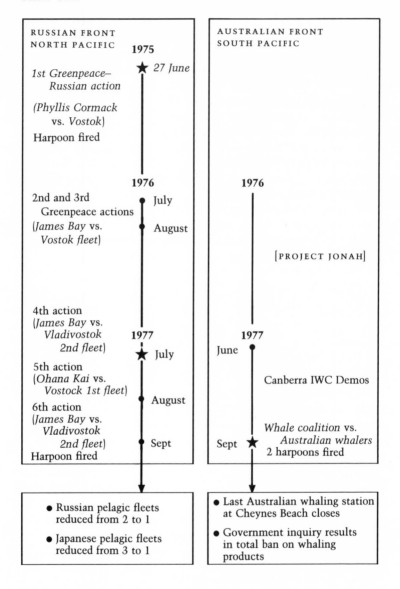

Figure 1.1 *The Pacific campaign 1975–77*

2

ECO-ESPIONAGE

1 THE SECRET AGENT

An army is only as effective as its knowledge of its enemy's tactics and movements allows it to be. So beside the direct action campaigns and political lobbyists and public campaigners, there was another kind of eco-warrior. He worked with equal dedication and courage, but realized the virtue of approaching warily and silently. This was the secret agent, the ecological detective.

The mantle of the chief eco-detective of the anti-whaling forces fell on the quiet and unassuming shoulders of a bearded and rather old-fashioned gentleman by the name of Nick Carter. A man who by his own admission likes to work behind the scenes, Carter has sat quietly through many an IWC conference biding his time, gathering and disseminating his intelligence, in his totally unlikely position as the non-governmental observer for the Assembly of Rabbis.

Working on his own initiative, but with the financial help of the International Society for the Protection of Animals at one time and as a director of the People's Trust for Endangered Species at another, Nick Carter has proved a formidable if unseen adversary to the whaling interests. Carter's soft-spoken, thoughtful manner is in tune with his quite religious belief in the sacred nature of life, but it belies his terrier-like determination and drive. Working through a network of contacts with seamen, sailors, maritime insurance companies, port authorities, shipping companies and financial institutions, as well as with activists and allies in numerous conservation organizations, and occasionally politicians and journalists, Nick Carter traced insurance and ownership documents, bills of lading, import and export documents and ships' records. Out of the staggering chaos and confusion of international shipping documentation, Carter's dogged persistence resulted in the stunning exposure of the single most destabilizing factor in the whole structure and working of the IWC: the unregulated, non-IWC whalers.

With the 30,000 to 40,000 whales being killed annually by the Japanese and Russians within the IWC, few environmentalists felt the issue of what went on outside the IWC membership of much significance. Nick Carter, however, was one observer who did not see it as a peripheral issue. With considerable insight and intuition, he believed that uncontrolled, unregulated whaling was being carried out secretly in order to circumvent IWC quotas. Furthermore, he believed it was being carried out at a level that was bound to undermine any attempt to protect endangered whale populations.

2 THE PIRATES

Even by the unruly standard of international whaling on the high seas, what Carter uncovered in his detective work was quite remarkable. He documented what the environmentalists later called 'the rise of the pirate whalers.'

If some initially objected to the use of the term 'pirate whaler', Carter's response was to expose a gang of modern outlaws whose operations flouted international laws and regulations, subverted international agreements and invaded national waters of many countries to plunder protected whale stocks. Armed with harpoon cannon and the whalers' long flensing blades, they were modern swashbuckling freebooters very much in the tradition of the rough old sea pirates.

Carter's investigations revealed a pirate ship and crew of the most flamboyant kind. The ship was a high-speed diesel killer boat that had been converted into a killer-factory ship with a rear slipway for slaughtering and with freezing compartments below. In short, she was a rather ingenious 'whaling-fleet-in-one' ship that since 1968 had, in various guises, zigzagged her way across the Atlantic, hunting continuously without control or restriction. The ship changed her name three times, from the *Robert W. Winke* to the *M.V. Run* to the *M.V. Sierra*. Her ownership shifted from the Netherlands to Norway to post box companies in Liechtenstein, the Bahamas, South Africa and Panama. She continually shifted her base of operations in numerous African and European ports, and in order to confuse matters even more, and move her beyond legal actions, she went through a stunning range of flag-of-convenience changes, from Dutch to Bahamian to Sierra Leonean to Somalian to Cypriot.

Carter's evidence showed that the ship had violated the fishing and whaling regulations of a score of countries. She illegally killed whales throughout the South Atlantic, an area where hunting was forbidden by the IWC. She was prosecuted in the Bahamas for illegal whaling, and later, in South Africa, bankruptcy proceedings by the Supreme Court were brought against her. She was forbidden entry into British-controlled ports. Once caught within two miles of the Nigerian shore by the coastguard with two whales in tow, the *Sierra* cut loose her kill, and threatening the Nigerian gunboat with her harpoon cannon, outran her pursuers. Twice run aground, twice bankrupted, she left behind unpaid fines of £20,000 and debts of a quarter of a million South African rand, yet like a phoenix she managed to rise each time from her ashes.

In the best (or worst) tradition of unruly pirate crews, there was an international cast of tough Norwegians, Africans, Indians, Portuguese and Japanese on the *Sierra*'s decks. And with shades of *Treasure Island*, she even had a mutiny of sorts. The Norwegian pirate captain, Knud Hansen, claimed that he had ended up with gunshot wounds, marooned and penniless, in the suitably remote port of Mocammedes in Angola, while his first mate and erstwhile partner Arvid Nordengen took over the ship and her crew.

Carter's investigations also revealed the whaling practices of the *Sierra*. The ship harpooned every whale that came within range. She took critically endangered species such as humpback, blue and right whales, and even killed undersized whales, nursing mothers and calves. She observed no closed season, but hunted at any time of year in any waters, whether protected areas or not. She operated without proper licence and reported only what she chose to be known of her operations.

She used the 'cold harpoon' whenever she could: that is, heavy harpoons *without* explosive grenade heads. This method of killing is cruel even when used to kill the smallest whale species, and when it is used on the larger species, the whale can take over three hours to die. Perhaps most shocking of all, the *Sierra* eventually found that it was most profitable to take the prime quality tail meat from the whale and simply dump the remaining 80 per cent of the whale carcass into the sea.

In terms of profitability, Carter had to admit that the Norwegian captains had quite brilliantly revised standard whaling practices. By their creative conversion of this killer ship into a killer-factory ship combine with deep-freezing storage, they managed to put into one ship several operations that had once required a small fleet. This miniaturizing of the industry at a time when the whale population as a whole had been reduced to about 10 per cent of its original population (while blue were at 4 per cent, humpback at 2 per cent and right at 1 per cent) allowed whalers to cost-effectively hunt very small whale populations. They could also hunt discreetly, without attracting much attention when they went into areas declared off limits.

In terms of whale conservation, the killer-factory ship was an unmitigated disaster. If such ships became common, every single whale the world over might be hunted down. Up until that time, perhaps the only thing that saved the decimated whale populations from having their last pockets of population wiped out was the fact that operating large pelagic whaling fleets proved too costly to be highly profitable when whales grew scarce. The downscaled industry of the pirates was just made to order for the 'final solution' for whales.

3 BLOWING COVER

In October 1975, Carter decided to go public with his information on the *Sierra* pirates. His carefully prepared report was sent to all IWC commissioners and observers. Furthermore, so it would not slip by unnoticed, he also broke the story in the world press, causing a considerable uproar.

With Carter's prompting, a journalist at the Cape Town *Argus* tracked down the ship's agent – Andrew Maurice Behr, director of the Sierra Fishing Company, South Africa. Behr was far from apologetic. He did not feel he had any obligation to be bound by the rules of the IWC, which he called a 'wishy-washy organization'. He could not see any reason not to hunt whales, endangered or not. After all, people came first, and he was providing jobs for people. What difference did it make? After all, he said, everyone knew 'whales are finished anyway'.

London's *Observer* chose to check out the registered owner whose name was supplied by Nick Carter. This was the Norwegian bank Forrentningsbanken. When contacted, the bank denied ownership. Their business was banking, they replied, not whaling. Later they admitted that, well, yes, they were the registered owners, but somewhat mystically this did not mean that the bank was 'in any way involved in whaling'. Four days after this inquiry, the ship's registered owners suddenly became an anonymous Beacon-Sierra Ltd, registered in Vaduz, Liechtenstein. From this new address, of course, no information whatever came forth, and certainly no admission of ownership or reports of whose money was backing the operation, either Norwegian or, as Carter suspected, Japanese.

Japan's Whaling Commission, despite its close ties with (not to say total control by) its whaling and fishing industry, denied any knowledge of the *Sierra*'s activities or the sale of its produce. It continued to proclaim this state of innocence even when confronted with copies of the *Sierra*'s meat production contract with the Taiyo Fishing Company (to which several of the delegation were closely linked), and with photos and names of the Japanese crew members on the *Sierra*. Photos were also presented of falsely labelled 'Fresh Frozen Whale Meat. Produce of Spain' being taken by the *Sierra* and loaded on to a Japanese cargo ship in the Canary Islands.

South Africa, fortunately, proved more capable of embarrassment as it had just that year declared an end to whaling. Also the *Sierra* had already been through the South African courts on previous prosecutions and there was new evidence that it had made false declarations to South African port authorities. Furthermore, Andrew Behr's comments were particularly offensive. The whole argument of the IWC's New Management Procedure was that through controlled exploitation of whales as a renewable resource, whales would thrive. The last thing the IWC wanted was a whaler saying whales didn't have a chance, let's finish them off quick and make big profits. South Africa had had enough of the *Sierra*.

However, the South African government stopped short of what Carter had hoped for, namely seizure by the authorities. Instead, it simply banned the vessel from South African waters. So, despite Agent Carter's work, the *Sierra* had not been stopped. Carter was not retiring from the field, however; at least the *Sierra* was denied South African as well as British ports, and with the Angolan war then raging she could not work in those waters, either. The pirates, with less and less in the way of sanctuary, moved northwards along the African coast. When the Somalian government was alerted to the *Sierra*'s activities, it appears that her flag-of-convenience was no longer convenient. Soon the *Sierra* became a Cypriot ship and continued her work unrepentant, but now at least on the run. From then on, the *Sierra* entered no records to the international whaling statisticians of whales killed, when at sea she never radioed her position, and when leaving port she never gave her destination.

But still, the bloody harvest continued.

3

THE WHALING COMMISSION

1 THE CLUB

The International Whaling Commission (IWC) was a 'whalers' club'. Like some exclusive big game shooting club, the members of the IWC since 1948 came together once a year before the opening of the killing season. They sat around a big table and smoked cigars, they had drinks in the bar and compared profits and talked of the good old days when the vast herds of great blue whales made life easy. Then they sat down at the table and bargained until they agreed among themselves what the sporting number of whales to be bagged this year would be. The quota was based on virtually non-existent science and a lot of wishful thinking. The hunt was a kind of 'gentlemen's agreement' between nations to abide by sporting rules: an exact date for the opening of the season, a ban on the killing of nursing mothers and undersized whales, and an immediate end to the killing when the quota was reached.

The trouble was that none of the gentlemen stuck to the agreement; and under the IWC direction more whales were killed than before its controls and regulations were set. There was no monitoring system of any accuracy to register violations, so-called observers were highly suspect, and if violations were by some accident revealed, there was no attempt to punish the transgressor.

Also, there were the non-members, like Aristotle Onassis, who did not even make a show of pretending to abide by the gentlemen's agreement. Clearly, perched on his whale penis barstool – his short little legs dangling – while cutting the throats of his competitors, Onassis was considered no gentleman. Besides his cut-throat tactics, many club members did not particularly like the company Onassis kept when he set up business in the 1950s. It particularly grated with the Norwegians, the great whaling nation of the time. The manager of the Onassis *Olympic Challenger* fleet was a disgraced member of the Norwegian Nazi Party; the company agent manager was the former administrator for Nazi Germany of the Norwegian whaling ships seized during the war; overall commander of the factory ship *Olympic Challenger* and its 17 killer boats was Captain Wilhelm Reichert, formerly of the Third Reich's navy; and most of the crew were German and ex-military. It turned out to be an ideal combination, of course, and they trounced the competition.

But when it came down to practicalities, there wasn't much to choose between the renegade Onassis and the IWC club members. The IWC members often violated their own set quotas, if it did not suit them, by simply filing an 'objection' and continuing the kill. In 1962 the USSR was suspected of having violated its Antarctic quota catch by some 5,000 humpback whales, but since it filed no report of them and no observers documented it, the violation remained unproved. In any case, there was no mechanism to sanction members for misbehaving.

The International Whaling Commission is an intergovernmental organization set up under the terms of the International Convention for the Regulation of Whaling (ICRW) in 1946. The Preamble to the ICRW states: 'The history of whaling has seen overfishing of one area after another to such a degree that it is essential to protect all species of whales from further overfishing.' To this end, the IWC, which first met in London in 1948, set limits on seasons and required the submission of catches and scientific data from whaling operations. The IWC was to set catch limits and whaling regulations and procedures.

It soon became apparent, however, that the ideal to 'safeguard for future generations the great natural resources represented by the whale stocks' was pushed to one side. In setting catch quotas, it was the capacity and requirements of the industry that were the priority. And predictably, the whale stocks grew smaller as the fleets grew bigger.

Under the aegis of the IWC during the 1950s and 1960s, more whales were killed than ever before. In 1933, when virtually no restrictions existed, 30,000 whales were killed; in 1962, under the IWC, nearly 67,000 whales were killed. By 1972, by which time whale stocks had long been decimated worldwide, quotas of well over 40,000 whales were still being granted. Before the IWC was formed three of the ten species of great whales were termed 'commercially extinct' – that is, too few to be worth the expense of hunting. These were right whales, bowheads and grey whales. Since then the IWC's controlled 'harvesting' programme has resulted in the commercial extinction of the blue, humpback, fin, sei and Bryde's whales, thus bringing the total to eight out of ten species. This is a policy of 'protection'!

When it came down to particulars, even in style and broad humour, it seems Onassis and many of the gentlemen whalers were not so far apart. Years after the Onassis whaling venture, one member of the IWC Scientific Committee boasted how, as a sly joke, he had made a present for a girlfriend. It was a beautiful white miniskirt. It was of very soft, seamless leather – made of exactly the same material as Mr Onassis's bar stools.

2 IN THE TRENCHES

The unanimous 52–0 nation vote for an immediate moratorium on all commercial whaling at the United Nations Environmental Conference in Stockholm, and the subsequent entrance of conservationist forces into the IWC conference in London two weeks later, signalled the real beginning of the Whale War.

However, when the conservationists marched bravely into the fray, they found their UN declaration with its resounding unanimous 52–0 vote had no force whatever within the IWC. For the whalers, the exercise of disposing of the conservationists proved about as strenuous as drowning kittens. The IWC was their club, after all. Whaling might be practised in the waters of some 41 nations, and there might only be 14 nations in the IWC, but those 14 considered themselves the sole judges of the fate of the whale.

The commissioners listened politely to the plea of the

Conservationists	Whalers
1972	1972–73 quota: 42,500
• **United Nations Proposal** of a 10 year moratorium on whaling. Vote: 52–0 • **US Marine Mammals Protection Act** protects whales and dolphins in US waters	• **IWC** in London – UN proposal rejected. Moratorium defeated Vote 4 yes / 6 no / 4 abstain
1973	1973–74 quota: 40,979
• **US Endangered Species Act** closes US markets and trade in whale products • **CITES – Convention In Trade of Endangered Species** International watchdog organization formed to close many international markets for whale products • **Pelly Amendment** to US Fishermen's Protection Act threatens trade embargo on Russia and Japan after IWC quota violations. This effectively makes the US IWC 'policeman'	• **IWC** – Moratorium fails again as ¾ majority necessary for passage Vote: 8 yes / 5 no / 1 abstains [**14 nations in IWC** – Japan, Russia, Iceland, Norway, South Africa in whalers block vote no. United States, Britain, Argentina, Mexico, Canada, France, Panama, Australia vote yes. Denmark abstains] • Russia and Japan violate IWC quotas by 3,000 whales each
1974	1974–75 quota: 39,864
• **New Management Procedure (NMP)** New IWC policy of 'scientific harvesting' of whales. Adopt 'sustained yield' basis of quotas. However database inadequate to implement NMP	• **IWC – 15 Nations** Japan makes ¾ majority vote virtually impossible by bringing in the Japanese-controlled Brazilian whalers
1975	1975–76 quota: 32,864
• 1st Greenpeace – Russian action in Pacific against *Vostok* fleet. Violations reported	• **IWC – Pirate Whaling Scandal** breaks implicating Japan, Norway, South Africa • South Africa stops whaling
1976	1976–77 quota: 28,050
• 2nd and 3rd Greenpeace – Russian actions. • **IWC – 16 Nations** – Conservationist New Zealand joins	• **IWC** – Loophole violations by Japan and Soviets, such as 'scientific permits'. Also massive increase in pirate whale meat imported into the Japanese market

Conservationists	Whalers
1977	1977–78 quota: 23,520
• 4th – 6th Greenpeace – Russian actions • Australian actions • **IWC – 17 Nations –** Conservationists Netherlands joins. • 2 Russian and 3 Japanese pelagic whaling fleets reduced to 1 fleet each.	• **'Eskimo Conspiracy'** – US abdicates role as IWC 'policeman' in order to win high quota of endangered bowhead whales for Alaskan Eskimos • **US 'Doublecross'** – at 'special' December meeting US allows Japan to increase sperm whale quota from 763 to 6,444.
1978	1978–79 quota: 20,428
• Greenpeace – Icelandic action	• **Pirate Whaling Epidemic** – Pirate whaling in Chile, Peru, Spain, Portugal, Taiwan, South Africa and Korea totally out of control. All are linked with Japan – making quota system meaningless and subverting New Management Procedure policy

Figure 3.1   The International Whaling Commission 1972–78

conservationist spokesmen. But when they voted, only four of the 14 nations supported the UN moratorium: America, Britain, Argentina and Mexico. Six voted against the moratorium and soundly trounced it: Japan, Russia, Norway, Iceland, South Africa and Panama. The remaining four, sensing no danger, simply abstained: Australia, Canada, Denmark and France.

It proved a mildly amusing diversion from the usual rather tedious division of spoils, but any real threat to Ahab's big game club seemed remote. By the time the 1973 IWC conference rolled around, the situation had changed dramatically. The intervening twelve months had seen the United States pass the Marine Mammal Protection Act and the revised US Endangered Species Act. These acts effectively closed America as a market for whale products. All use and importation of whale products was banned, and all hunting – with the exception of aboriginals – forbidden. It was also the year when the watchdog Convention In Trade Of Endangered Species (CITES) was formed to monitor and stop the international trade in endangered species and commerce in products made from them. It was a year in the wake of the UN vote in which lobbyists enlisted many influential politicians in the European Common Market (EEC) and throughout the world to ban whaling and whale products.

However, it was an obscure piece of American legislation that made the real difference. The Pelly Amendment to the Fishermen's Protection Act made it possible to *embargo* all fish and wildlife products from any nation that 'diminishes the effectiveness of an international fishery or wildlife conservation agreement'. It was the only act that could be used to give teeth to IWC rulings internationally.

When the Japanese and Russian quotas for 1973 were violated by more than 3,000 whales each, American President Ford immediately issued an ultimatum: any further objections to or violations of IWC quotas would result in the invocation of the Pelly Amendment. Suddenly outright defiance of the IWC began to look too costly. For Japan in particular, it might cost hundreds of millions of dollars. For several years to come this single piece of legislation was the main deterrent in preventing the Japanese and Soviets challenging IWC quotas. The United States had effectively become the IWC's policeman.

So when the crunch came and the moratorium vote was called for at the 1973 IWC, it was a very different story from the year before. This time it was the whalers who were reeling from the impact.

The count was eight yes votes to five no votes, and one abstention. The four yes votes of 1972 for the moratorium were joined by three former abstainers; and amazingly Panama deserted the whalers' ranks and also voted yes. Only Denmark abstained. It was a clear majority for the moratorium. But the IWC had not been a whalers' club since 1948 for nothing. Any restrictive ruling in the IWC required not just a simple majority, but a three-quarter majority vote. And this the conservation nations had narrowly failed to achieve.

However, the whalers' club was shaken to its foundations. Forever after, the whalers were doomed to be a minority voice within their own convention.

3 BAD YEARS

Although the trench war of the IWC was less spectacular than the eco-guerillas' raids on the whaling fleets, most conservationists saw it as the most critical battleground. Only the IWC, they believed, could bring about a negotiated end to the Whale War.

However by 1974 the possibility of victory by surprise attack had been lost, and both sides were deeply entrenched. Furthermore, Japan had rigged the voting by recruiting Brazil as an IWC nation. For some time Brazil had been the base of a Japanese-owned and -managed whaling station that worked illegally outside the rules and quotas of the IWC. This had suited its Japanese owners and allowed them to hunt critically endangered species without detection. Now, however, Brazil's whaling commissioner served very nicely as a Japanese puppet when it came to moratorium ruling.

The entrance of Brazil into the IWC ended any immediate chance that a three-quarter vote might be achieved. However, in order to placate public outcry and American pressure, the 1974 IWC ushered in a new strategy called the New Management Procedure (NMP).

Once again the IWC recanted and lamented the policies of exploitation and greed in the industry which resulted in the past destruction of whale stocks. Once again it promised a fresh start with the NMP. No longer, the whalers proclaimed – hand on heart – would the dictates of the industry argue for quotas; quotas would now be set according to a 'scientific' evaluation of whale stocks. For the first time, 'management' of whale stocks would be attempted on a 'sustainable yield' basis. That is, the whalers argued, they would take no more whales each year than could be naturally replaced by population growth. Catch quotas would be set stock by stock, and species by species.

It soon became apparent that the NMP required adequate catch and biological data, a database on original populations and studies of population dynamics of each species. None of this was undertaken. Catch quotas remained optimistic fantasies, and the populations continued to decline.

Meanwhile, Japanese and Russian strategists managed to find legal loopholes as a means of exceeding quotas by many thousands of whales without appearing to directly challenge the IWC's authority. By intentionally 'misunderstanding' rulings, issuing unilateral 'scientific permits' and hunting unclassified species such as orcas, the whalers managed to supplement their quotas by several thousand whales.

Each year environmentalists presented the IWC with evidence

of scores of violations by every member whaling nation. At the very least, every whaling nation was found to incidentally, but consistently, violate the minimum-size rule.

Unbelievably, since the IWC official independent 'observer' scheme supposedly began in 1972, not one violation of any substance was ever reported. In most cases these observers either were inadequately represented or did not exist at all. Some others, such as those on Russian and Japanese factory ships, seemed to completely lack any kind of perceptive faculties, and their data could not be trusted. (Conveniently, the Russian fleet had two Japanese observers, and the Japanese fleet had two Russian observers.)

As Craig van Note's Washington-based environmental consortium Monitor stated:

Without exception every whaling operation in the world is, in some form or another, violating the regulations, principles or quotas which are the basis of the international attempt to 'conserve' or 'manage' whales. . . . At the heart of the continued violations of the IWC's quota system is the ineffective observer scheme. The present system is so incomplete and lacking both in resources and personnel that it hardly exists.

Not once has the IWC ever acted upon any violation of its own rules. Environmental groups registered violations simply to get them on the public record, but the IWC did not attempt even the most basic sanction such as the deduction of whales killed over the previous year's quota from the number to be killed in the new year. Consequently, despite the widespread and highly visible actions of the Save the Whale movement, and the steady reduction of quotas and territories that were open to the IWC whaling nations, 1974 to 1978 were bad years for the whales. The New Management Procedure was proving a total failure, and it was debatable whether quotas were sinking because of anti-whaling pressure or simple depletion of whale numbers.

During this time, Sir Peter Scott, speaking for the World Wildlife Fund, addressed the IWC commissioners. Scott instructed the assembly that despite the proposed New Management Procedure and the quota systems of the IWC, whale populations were continuing to decline. It was absolute proof that no effort at all was made to have a 'sustained yield' balance of the whale stocks. 'It seems,' Scott concluded, 'that whaling is likely to continue unabated until all whale stocks are commercially extinct. This will be the ultimate indictment of the IWC and its policy.'

4 THE AMERICAN DOUBLE-CROSS

By December 1977 there was very bad news indeed at the IWC. It was becoming evident that America was not acting convincingly in its role as the IWC policeman. The environmentalists started to sense a double-cross in the making. The new US commissioner was Richard Frank, whom most folk with conservationist leanings found unsympathetic in the extreme. The strong conservationist stance of the US started to fade, and under 'Big Dick' Frank the use of the Pelly Amendment as a threat seemed less and less likely.

While publicly, President Carter – with the encouragement of Congressmen such as Don Bonker and Paul McCloskey, as well as Senators Warren Magnusson and Bob Packwood – advocated a total cessation of whaling, Dick Frank was up to all sorts of closed-door meetings with the Japanese and the Soviets. On the one hand President Carter was saying, 'I am wholeheartedly committed to strong action to guarantee the survival of the great whales.' On the other, Dick Frank was voicing his attitudes to a *Washington Post* interviewer during an IWC meeting: 'Frank criticized militant conservationists and anti-whaling countries for being "unrealistic and inflexible" in their uncompromising demands for a total ban on whaling. . . . "We have to attempt to accommodate them," Frank said, "and I believe we can do it in the relatively near future." '

The degree to which Dick Frank accommodated the Japanese astonished everybody. Furthermore, after the change from the Carter to the Reagan administration resulted in Frank's removal as IWC commissioner, that memorable phrase 'even paranoids have enemies' came to mind for more than one conservationist. The worst suspicions of the most paranoid environmentalist seemed confirmed. Frank became officially registered as a 'foreign agent', a lobbyist and adviser with a retainer of $73,000. He was personally hired by his supposed adversary at the IWC, the Japanese whaling commissioner Kunio Yonezawa.

However, it was not just Big Dick's natural talent for making backroom deals that was behind the US abdication as leader and enforcer of the international drive to save the whales. It was, as might be expected, internal American politics. It was a controversy that was to tie Americans in knots, and the result would be that America would never fully recover its once clear stance on the whaling issue. The controversy was the 'Eskimo factor', which might be bitterly summed up by a glance at the angry black humour emblazoned on T-shirts sold by Eskimo shops in Anchorage and Nome: 'Save a whale – eat an Eskimo.'

5 THE ESKIMO CONSPIRACY

In the Arctic waters of Alaska, there swims the most severely endangered of all whale species, the great bowhead whale. It is a magnificent animal, 60 feet in length, 80 tons in weight, with an enormous arch-shaped mouth like a cathedral door big enough for two elephants to stand in side by side. Inside its mouth are some 300 pairs of baleen plates about 13 feet long used for feeding on plankton.

It was primarily for these baleen plates that the bowhead whale was hunted in Alaskan waters from 1850 to 1913. Whalebone (baleen) was sold at $6 a pound for ladies' corsets, skirt hoops, buggywhips, umbrellas, and so on – and each whale provided a ton of baleen. The population originally estimated at 62,000 was reduced by 1913 to less than 4,000. Commercial whaling of the bowhead ceased because there were too few animals left to make an Arctic voyage worthwhile.

Between 1913 and 1970 Alaskan Eskimos continued their traditional bowhead hunts, taking from 10 to 20 whales each year. This was certainly a peripheral issue. The IWC had until the 1970s dealt only with commercial whaling, and the kill rate was small even though the population has never recovered from the terrible devastation of the nineteenth-century whaling. The bowhead population remained at between 3,000 and 4,000 animals, and seems to have a growth rate of only a tenth of 1 per cent, or perhaps 30 to 40 whales per year.

In the 1970s there began a disastrous increase in Eskimo hunting: from fewer than 20 a year as many as 100 were being killed. In 1976 48 bowheads were killed and landed, and another 43 struck and lost, and undoubtedly died. In 1977 26 were killed and landed while 78 others were struck and lost. The bowheads fell to an all-time population low – perhaps 2,000 to 3,000 – and conservationists called for a halt to the slaughter.

The whale hunt is a prestige event in Eskimo society. Until recently, only the village elders were allowed to captain a whale boat and control the use of the grenade lances that have replaced the hand harpoons. However, with the new wealth that Alaskan oil has brought, the number of crews and boats has doubled and many young men suddenly took to the hunt. Having served no lengthy apprenticeship they proved extremely inefficient killers, and harpooned far more whales than could be justified. Also, the killing of mature prime breeding female bowheads was often recorded – a policy that invited further rapid population decline.

Under normal circumstances, it would be a clear-cut matter of applying the Endangered Species Act to the obviously endangered bowheads. However, in American law native Indians and Eskimos as subsistence hunters are exempt from such restrictions. The terrible irony, of course, is that aboriginal hunting could never have endangered the bowhead on its own; it was the nineteenth-century Yankee whalers who primarily destroyed the population in the first place. Furthermore, a good deal of national guilt was involved, for without doubt, historically, the aboriginal people have themselves been as ill-used as the bowheads by the Americans.

It was naturally easy for Alaskan Senators and Congressmen to argue solely for a limit to 'commercial' whaling and turn a blind eye to 'aboriginal' whaling. It was, after all, a major voters' issue for Alaskans. Naturally enough too, the Scientific Committee of the IWC found it almost impossible to ignore this as a simple aboriginal hunt since, at the present kill rate, in a very few years the bowhead would become biologically extinct – not simply 'commercially extinct'. As it was, even without the Eskimo hunt, many wondered if the bowhead population would ever recover anyway.

The whaling nations now grasped with both hands the perfect opportunity to incapacitate the American conservation effort. They voted for a total banning of bowheads 15–0 with one US abstention, in the IWC Scientific Committee meeting. Then Japan and the other whalers began a horse-trading session with the Americans – sperm whale for bowheads – in the closed-door commissioners' meeting at the IWC. From that time onwards,

America found itself unable to argue for a moratorium on whaling. Instead it found itself, against its own and IWC scientific advice, fighting primarily for the highest possible bowhead quota for the Eskimos.

The currency of the convention changed to that of bowheads, one bowhead to 200 or so sperm whales. Catching the US between the Save the Whale lobby and the Save the Vote in Alaska lobby, the whaling nations managed to neutralize their greatest foe. As Senator Paul McCloskey said after his attendance at the 1977 IWC conference, when he spoke forcefully for the acceptance of the zero quota ruling:

> Only the United States has the combination of resources, motivation and bargaining power to force other nations to give up the economic benefit involved. . . . Should the United States be unable to accept and implement the IWC's ruling on the bowhead, we can scarcely expect to maintain our credibility in any position of conservation leadership with the Japanese or the Russians.

A letter to President Carter signed by 67 conservation groups stated the case flatly:

> The US has abdicated leadership in the international effort to end commercial whaling because the US commissioner to the IWC has given priority to obtaining a high quota for Alaska's Eskimos on the endangered bowhead whale. The US must not compromise its principles by trading off hundreds and thousands of whales to the commercial whaling nations for a handful of bowhead whales. Please direct our IWC commissioner to adhere to your commendable policy against commercial whaling and to oppose all secret meetings at the IWC.

Sometimes, the saying goes, in Washington the ears have walls. This was one such case. 'Big Dick' Frank remained addicted to secret meetings and bowhead poker. Late in 1977 at a 'special' December meeting in Tokyo, in exchange for his handful of bowheads Frank allowed an *increase* in sperm whale quotas to go from 763 (as agreed at the general meeting) to an astonishing 6,444.

The Eskimo-bowhead controversy proved to be the most deeply divisive issue in the conservationist camp for several years to come. The conservationist ideals of the US commission were washed out on the tide of Alaskan votes.

6 PLAGUE OF PIRATES

During these dark years, bad news within the IWC was matched by absolutely terrible news outside its sphere. Nick Carter, the dogged eco-detective, had hoped that his exposure in 1975 of the pirate whaler *Sierra* would bring about an end to its activities and that the resulting publicity would make pirate whale meat too hot to be bought by IWC nations. On all counts Nick Carter was proved wrong. By 1978 he and a network of eco-espionage investigators had uncovered an unbelievable international conspiracy.

The *Sierra* had in fact inspired a whole generation of pirates. By 1978 the single example of the *Sierra* had exploded into pirate whaling operations worldwide, set up through dummy companies with post box addresses. Others were set up with government permission, flying flags-of-convenience, as national industries, but were in fact financed, managed and controlled by the Japanese – as was the case in Brazil, which the environmentalists labelled 'a Japanese whaling colony'. By 1978, Nick Carter and a network of eco-espionage investigators had uncovered an unbelievable international conspiracy. In Chile a Japanese pirate ship registered with a dummy Panamanian company was slaughtering whales in coastal waters. In Peru three Japanese pirate ships were killing year round in Peruvian territorial waters. In Taiwan a fleet of four pirate whalers was decimating whale herds in the South China Sea. Korean pirates were at work in the Sea of Japan, and in the North Atlantic a fleet of four Spanish pirate whalers continued their unrestricted slaughter.

Adding insult to injury, the *Sierra* had resurfaced in the Canary Islands. Not only did she continue to hunt but she had been joined by a sister ship, the *Tonna*. Furthermore, Carter was astonished to find that a fleet of no fewer than three more pirate ships was being fitted in South Africa by the interests behind the *Sierra*, in order to massively expand operations.

Pirate whaling operations had reached an epidemic level. Cynical opportunists were making their fortunes with impunity. Clearly, pirate whaling was out of control and was subverting the

IWC quota system. This, on top of Japanese and Russian violations, the Eskimo conspiracy and the American double-cross, spelled disaster for the future of the whales.

The situation was explosive. Something had to be done.

PART TWO

'Believe ye, men, in things called omens?

CAPTAIN AHAB in Moby Dick

4

NEMESIS

1 THE WHITE WHALES

In the whaling season of 1957 a Japanese harpoon boat pursued a kind of ghostly apparition through the Pacific swells. The big diesel engines pushed the steel hull relentlessly after the tiring whale, and the chase took its fatal mechanical course. The harpooner fired, the shot exploded in the water before him, there was a bloody whirlpool as the whale sounded. The crew played out the harpoon cable, the whale struggled, and finally the winch and cable won out, and the whale came up dying, its jaws gaping wide.

When at last the whale lay upon the flensing deck, even the factory ship workers, who butchered whales by the thousand each year, hesitated. For what lay before them to be slaughtered was a most unusual creature – a snow-white sperm whale. The whale was carefully measured and examined. Exact notations were made. Then finally the butchering began. Beneath the skin, this was just another whale.

But I wonder: did the whalers, as they stood for a time with the long razors of their flensing knives at their sides, perceive in the whale 'the white gliding ghostliness' of which Melville spoke in *Moby Dick*? Was there something 'in allusion to the white, silent stillness of death'? For beyond Melville's story there has always been something about albinism that has struck a deep inner chord, and tales of wrathful white whales as the nemesis of whalers had come into being long before *Moby Dick*.

It seems everyone in the whaling industry knows something of Melville's white whale, even among the Japanese, for when cetologist Ohsumi wrote a scientific paper on the 1957 killing of the white whale, the title was inevitably 'A Descendant of Moby Dick, or A White Sperm Whale'.

The white whale was, as Ohsumi wrote, 'not so gigantic or grotesque as Moby Dick'. In fact, it was a juvenile male sperm whale just over half-grown at 35 feet; Ohsumi wrote with certain hints of romance and sadness, 'If it had not been killed in young generation, it would have reigned over the sea in future like the ancestor Moby Dick'.

White sperm whales were not unknown outside fiction, although a pure white animal had never before been recorded as being killed. In 1950, the Japanese caught a sperm whale with a white head, jaw and belly; in 1972 the Soviets reported a very pale, pink-eyed sperm whale taken by their vessels. However, none of these whales possessed that inner hateful wrath towards men that Melville's legend attributed to his great white sperm whale. Still, there was one historic albino whale who *did* possess exactly those qualities. His name was Mocha Dick.

2 MOCHA DICK AND THE AVENGERS

In the May 1839 issue of *The Knickerbocker, New York Monthly Magazine*, there appeared a factual article written by J. N. Reynolds about a whale that had for some years made whaling in the Pacific a considerable hazard for its pursuers. This dangerous bull sperm whale had been named after an island off the Chilean coast – Mocha Island – where it was most commonly encountered. Reynolds's article, written a dozen years before *Moby Dick*, was entitled *Mocha Dick, or The White Whale of the Pacific*.

There can be little doubt that Melville had either read the article or had heard from other whalemen the legend of this same whale that attacked boats. The prototype Moby Dick certainly seems to have been a real whale, and Reynolds described him as 'white as wool'. When he leapt full out of the water in a frenzied rage, 'the falling mass was white as a snowdrift.'

This living avalanche gave Melville's book its central image and the object of the quest, but Melville worked hard to make us know that the whale's whiteness was but an outward sign of an inwardly even more freakish nature, a figure of dangerous, raging retribution. In those days of wooden ships and hand-held harpoons, there were such whales – though always rare, it is true. When a herd was struck, the bull would often turn on the whalers to defend the cows and their young. And many a whaler found his nemesis in the form of a charging sperm whale, and as the whaler Captain Charles Scammon wrote in those times, the most dangerous were those 'vicious, grey-headed old Cachalots'.

As Melville knew well enough, retribution need not wear an outward sign. In 1850, the year before Melville completed *Moby Dick*, a black bull sperm whale marked only by an inner wrathful, freakish nature (an albinism of the spirit) turned upon the whaler *Ann Alexander*. The black bull rammed the *Ann Alexander*, stove her in and sank her in the whaling grounds off the coast of Peru.

But the real prototype of Melville's *Pequod* was not the *Ann Alexander*, it was the Nantucket whaler the *Essex*, which was likewise rammed and sunk by a black bull sperm whale. Melville is known to have met the son of Owen Chase, the first mate aboard the ship. Chase had survived three months adrift in a small boat, despite starvation and dehydration – and eventual cannibalism of some of the crew. Owen Chase's title left no room for equivocation: *Narrative of the Shipwreck of the Whale Ship* Essex *of Nantucket, Which Was Attacked and Finally Destroyed by a Large Sperm Whale in the Pacific Ocean. By Owen Chase of Nantucket, First Mate of Said Vessel.* It was from Chase's narrative that Melville undoubtedly conceived the end of his own tale, and for over 160 years it remained the only known account of the sinking of the *Essex*. However, in 1981, a 100-page journal written by Thomas Nickerson, a 16-year-old cabin boy aboard the *Essex*, was discovered in an attic in Connecticut and sent to Edouard Stackpole, curator of the Nantucket Peter Foulger Museum.

In Nickerson's description of the disaster, on 20 November 1820 the *Essex* was in the mid-Pacific and her crews were out killing whales where a bull sperm whale was causing some havoc. Nickerson was aboard the 238-ton mother ship at this time and reported the incident:

I being then at the helm and looking on the windward side of the ship saw a very large whale approaching us. I called out to the mate to inform him of it. On his seeing the whale he instantly gave me an order to put the helm hard up. I had scarcely time to obey the order when I heard a loud cry from several voices at once, that the whale was coming foul of the ship. Scarcely had the sound of their voices reached my ears when it was followed by a tremendous crash, the whale had struck the ship with his head under the larboard fore chains at the water's edge with such force as to shock every man upon his feet. The whale then getting under the ship's bottom came up under the starboard quarters. . . . The monster took a turn off about 300 yards ahead, then turning short came around with his utmost speed and again struck the ship a tremendous blow with his head and with such force as to stove in the whole bow at the water's edge. One of the men who was below at the time came running upon deck saying 'The ship is filling with water.' We turned our attention to getting clear the boat, the only boat left with us, with which we could expect escape.

In 1867 the Norwegian whaler Svend Foyn invented the grenade harpoon which was fired from a small cannon. The following year he equipped a steam-powered ship with his new weapon and the modern era of whaling began. It was not particularly fast off the mark, and for a long time the Norwegians were ahead of everyone in technology. Before the twentieth century and the really massive slaughter that began with the opening of the Antarctic whaling grounds, there was a real mixture of primitive and high-tech whaling.

However, by the turn of the century nearly all major whaling nations used steam-powered, steel-hulled ships with cannon and grenade harpoons. These made counterattack by whales a futile effort, and escape almost impossible, even for the once untouchably fast great blue, fin and sei whales.

This is not to say whales (or, specifically, sperm whales) ceased to attack the huge new steel ships, but the exploding harpoon ensured that in so doing they would die all the more quickly. The extraordinary power of the great whales is evident in the incident of the non-whaling, steel-hulled steamer *Seminole* which, in 1896, sailed from New York to Jacksonville. The steamer was sailing full speed ahead when she accidently crossed paths with a pod of a dozen sperm whales. The steel hull of the *Seminole* sheered into the back of a whale cow, 'causing billows of bloody spume to explode'. The wounded cow either sank or dove deep and away from the steamer, but the bull of the herd immediately rammed the vessel so severely that passengers were knocked off their feet, and furniture and machinery were shaken from their fittings. The bull did not strike just the once, but four times. It had struck 'loosening steel hull plates' until 'seawater was seeping through the ruptures'. Fortunately for the *Seminole*, the whale was either exhausted by his efforts or his rage had sufficiently abated for him to allow the steamer to flee. One more ramming might very well have sunk the ship.

So it was that steel walls, harpoon cannons and harpoons with explosive heads, commonplace by the turn of the century, rendered impotent the once ominous vengeance of a retaliatory 'Moby Dick'. Man's massive and deadly technology now dwarfed the size and power of even the largest of the earth's creatures. Or so it seemed.

3 1978 REMAKE OF *MOBY DICK*

By 1978 duplicity within the IWC had reached its deepest trough, and pirate whaling had reached colossal proportions. A time of retribution for the whalers, particularly the ruthless pirates, was long overdue. The tide of the Whale War was changing, and if any whalers that year were looking for an omen of the future course of the war, they would find one in the tale of the pirate whaler *M.V. Tonna*.

The 543-ton *Tonna* entered the pirate armada of the North Atlantic in a series of devious transformations typical of all pirate whaling vessels. She was once the Japanese trawler *Shunyo Maru*. Then she appeared in Curacao in the Caribbean as the *Southern Fortune*. By the time she finally joined the *Sierra* (her now notorious sister pirate vessel) in the Canaries, she was named the *M.V. Tonna* and had been converted into a whaler. Typically, she was registered not as a whaler but as a fishing boat under the dummy company Red Mullet Fishing and flew the Netherlands Antilles flag-of-convenience – or, more to the point, flag-of-confusion. By chance, its managers happened to be the now familiar Sierra Fishing Agency, a division of the quotable Andrew M. Behr of South Africa.

The *Tonna* combined operations with the *Sierra*, sometimes acting as the *Sierra*'s factory ship because of her larger slipway, and sometimes killing and slaughtering the whales herself. The result was that the ships had doubled their killing range and doubled their tonnage. Together they continued to kill every species they encountered, and cut only the prime meat from them, dumping the rest back into the sea.

On 27 June 1978 the *Tonna* made a solo whaling voyage; the *Sierra* was laid up in port with repairs. By 22 July she was returning to the Canaries with her freezers packed with 450 tons of whale meat. Weighted down as she was, the *Tonna* rode very low in the water. Some 220 miles off Portugal, at about five o'clock in the evening, the *Tonna* sighted a sleek 70-foot fin whale. Her Norwegian captain, Kristhof Vesprhein, succumbed to pure greed. He accelerated the engines to full diesel power and overtook the enormous fin whale. The harpooner fired into the beast and played the steel line with the powerful winch as the whale dove and thrashed in the water, slowly dying.

As the whale fought on, and the *Tonna* struggled to pull in her prey, deep sea swells rapidly rose up and began to pitch the heavily laden ship from side to side. Suddenly, while the crew attempted to drag the 50-ton whale on to the slipway, the whale's weight and a large swell pulled the ship far over to one side. The overladen *Tonna* keeled over, the rail was pushed under water, the scuppers were awash. Because of the tropical heat, several hatches and portholes had been carelessly left open in the stern, and the sea poured in. The engine room flooded, blowing out all the electrics. Not only was there no engine power but the winches were immobilized. The crew could neither release their catch nor cut it loose.

The ship became the captive of the captured whale, the two wrapped in a fatal embrace. The swift fin whale, known as the greyhound of the sea, was now a deadly 50-ton anchor pulling the destroyer down with it. As its grey back rolled away, its long white belly turned up. The weight of the fin whale tugged the line again, the sea rushed in faster, the speed of descent accelerated, and that colourful international cast of 42 pirate whalers rushed for the lifeboats.

What happened next cannot be easily explained. Captain

Kristhof Vesprhein refused to give up the fight, and despite appeals from his crew would not abandon his ship. Like one in a dream, mesmerized, he refused to leave the bridge. Something else tugged at him as the whale tugged on the ship. Did he see in the white belly of the whale an old tale, its time come around again: the great whale pulling him and all the machinery of death at his command into the beckoning vortex of oblivion? Adamant, resigned to fate, he remained on the bridge – a beer bottle in his hand – and waved his crew away.

The *Tonna* pitched again and the 50-ton whale pulled the ship, her 450-ton cargo, her arsenal of harpoons and cannon and her pirate captain down to a watery grave. And just as Melville concluded his tale over a century before, when the whirling vortex of the ship subsided, 'the great shroud of the sea rolled on as it rolled five thousand years ago.'

For the pirates of the Atlantic, it was an ill omen. It was a warning of worse to come. The tide of their war had changed, and all their luck was gone. The 42 survivors of the *Tonna* were rescued that same night just before midnight by a Greek freighter to which had been relayed the *Tonna's* distress call. On her decks, the orphaned crewmen told their rescuers a strange variation of that old tale of Moby Dick, and how they had lost their own Ahab and his ship to the whale.

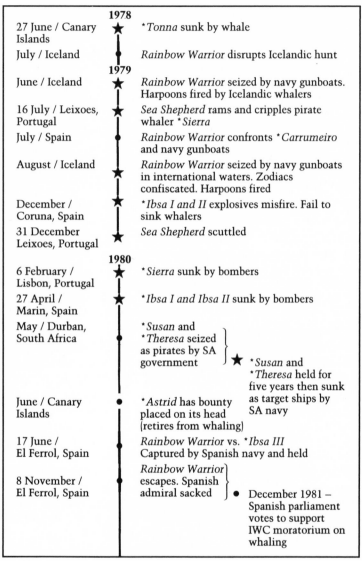

1978

27 June / Canary Islands ★ *Tonna* sunk by whale

July / Iceland *Rainbow Warrior* disrupts Icelandic hunt

1979

June / Iceland ★ *Rainbow Warrior* seized by navy gunboats. Harpoons fired by Icelandic whalers

16 July / Leixoes, Portugal ★ *Sea Shepherd* rams and cripples pirate whaler *Sierra

July / Spain *Rainbow Warrior* confronts *Carrumeiro and navy gunboats

August / Iceland *Rainbow Warrior* seized by navy gunboats in international waters. Zodiacs confiscated. Harpoons fired

December / Coruna, Spain ★ *Ibsa I and II explosives misfire. Fail to sink whalers

31 December Leixoes, Portugal ★ *Sea Shepherd* scuttled

1980

6 February / Lisbon, Portugal ★ *Sierra sunk by bombers

27 April / Marin, Spain ★ *Ibsa I and Ibsa II sunk by bombers

May / Durban, South Africa *Susan and *Theresa seized as pirates by SA government ★ *Susan and *Theresa held for five years then sunk as target ships by SA navy

June / Canary Islands *Astrid has bounty placed on its head (retires from whaling)

17 June / El Ferrol, Spain *Rainbow Warrior* vs. *Ibsa III Captured by Spanish navy and held

8 November / El Ferrol, Spain *Rainbow Warrior* escapes. Spanish admiral sacked December 1981 – Spanish parliament votes to support IWC moratorium on whaling

* Whalers

Figure 4.1 Atlantic blitz 1978–80

5

BLITZKRIEG

1 NORTH ATLANTIC SQUADRON

Within days of the sinking of the *Tonna*, the first eco-warship in the North Atlantic is launched. She is painted green and white and her bow is decorated with a rainbow and a white dove. She is called the *Rainbow Warrior*.

The launching of the *Rainbow Warrior* in 1978 was something of a small miracle in itself, and in no small part due to the efforts of Canadian activist Allan Thornton. Tall and straight with clean-cut features and a sometimes severe glance, Thornton would not have made a bad Canadian Mountie recruit if it were not for his innate ecologist's phobia for uniforms. In 1976 Thornton came to England and, financing the venture himself, attempted to set up the first Greenpeace office in Europe.

Not content with the turmoil Greenpeace was creating in the Pacific, he and a few others felt it was time to launch new campaigns in the Atlantic theatre of the Whale War. He felt it was essential that Europeans became aware of the continued slaughter of whales just off their shores.

There were ecology groups who were strong Save the Whale campaigners in Europe: Friends of the Earth, the World Wildlife Fund, Project Jonah, the RSPCA and the International Society for the Protection of Animals. However, none of these groups had yet developed the headline-grabbing eco-guerilla tactics of

Greenpeace that Thornton thought essential for the Whale War.

Although Greenpeace had received considerable press coverage and even praise for its actions in England, Thornton found virtually no funding forthcoming from either the public or from other environmental groups. Thornton had to resort to sleeping on other people's floors. He was down to his last two pounds when he by chance wrote a letter to the *Guardian* after an article praising Greenpeace appeared in its pages. The letter simply pointed out that all this patting on the back was well and good, but the financing of these acts of heroism had to come from somewhere. Was there anyone out there who might think it worthwhile to reward Greenpeace's London office with a donation of more than words of praise?

Indeed there was. Thornton's letter in fact triggered off one of the stranger twists in the ecology movement's history. For the letter provoked a reply from a totally unexpected source, and the salvation of Greenpeace's only European office at that moment, and its continued sustenance for the following year, was almost entirely due to the good grace of one comedian and four pop stars. The comedian was Spike Milligan, who on reading Thornton's letter telephoned and then met him. The four pop stars were none other than the Beatles, who at Milligan's instigation were persuaded to the nobility of the cause.

Through the generosity of Milligan and the Beatles, Thornton was able to set up a proper office and incorporate Greenpeace-UK in May 1977. This began a chain of events which resulted in a Greenpeace-France being established in Paris by ex-Project Jonah activist Remi Parmentier, and still later the Greenpeace-Netherlands, followed by organizations in Germany and Denmark.

David McTaggert, the Greenpeace activist who had challenged French authority by sailing into its nuclear test zone in the Pacific, had been in Europe for some time. A tough and able campaigner with considerable organizational skill. McTaggert soon took the helm of Greenpeace-Europe, and shortly after that the entire Greenpeace-International organization came under his control.

Meanwhile in Britain, within months of incorporating Greenpeace-UK, Thornton was negotiating for the purchase of a Greenpeace ship. This was finally made possible by a World Wildlife Fund-Netherlands grant of £45,000. So in July 1978 the *Rainbow Warrior* was launched and with it, by sailing against the Icelandic whalers in the North Atlantic, a new front in the Whale War.

The *Rainbow Warrior* remained in Icelandic waters for a month, frustrating all attempts at whaling. The conflict proved grudging, but there was no violence. However by the second campaign in 1979 the Icelandic attitude had hardened. Showing even less regard for human life than other whaling fleets, the whalers aboard the *Hvalur* ships fired a total of *five* harpoons at close range over the Greenpeace floating pickets. Still the Greenpeace tactics proved to be remarkably successful in thwarting the whalers in their work.

As a result, a new dimension arose in the Whale War: armed naval escorts for whalers. The Icelandic government sent in its navy gunboats and escalated the conflict. The *Rainbow Warrior* was twice seized by gunboats. The second confrontation took place in international waters where the ship was illegally boarded and had her Zodiac inflatables stripped from her.

In the midst of the Icelandic conflict, the *Rainbow Warrior* made a sudden strike on the Spanish whaling fleet. Spain, unlike Iceland, was a non-IWC nation and made no pretence of even appearing to observe whaling quotas or restrictions. Even the most basic rulings, such as not hunting critically endangered blue and humpback whales, were ignored.

The *Rainbow Warrior* tracked down the Spanish whaling tug, the *Carrumeiro* of the Juan Masso fleet, and succeeded in harassing her attempts at whaling off Cape Finisterre for several days. Like the Icelanders, the Spaniards soon called in a navy gunboat, and for another day the *Rainbow Warrior* and her Zodiacs persisted in a game of cat and mouse. Again the tactics proved successful and the gunboat not wishing to exert extreme force, left the next day in frustration. Satisfactorily, the *Carrumeiro* also withdrew from the conflict.

These encounters, as it turned out, were just the initial skirmishes in the Atlantic theatre of the Whale War. The fight was only just beginning. It would soon prove to be the hottest battleground in the entire war.

2 THE KAMIKAZE

It was just after 1 o'clock on a Sunday afternoon, in mid-July

1979 when a crewman pointed out a pale, distant ship to the captain of the pirate whaler the *Sierra*. The crew always kept an eye out for other ships, particularly when they were whaling. On this day, though, the *Sierra* was not whaling. Indeed, she had just completed several weeks' hunting and was now returning to port with her freezers packed with half a million dollars' worth of whale meat. Captain Nordengen was relaxed; despite all the publicity over the *Sierra*'s activities and the sinking of the *Tonna*, profits would be good again this year. To throw off nosy environmentalists, the *Sierra* had changed her base of operations from the Canaries to Portugal, and news was coming through that the company was acquiring three new ships to expand the pirate fleet.

A couple of hours passed before Nordengen realized that the ship on the horizon was not passing, but was in fact following him. He did not know what it was about, but he did not like it and pushed full throttle ahead. But the pale ship was fast, moving up on the *Sierra* at what must have been close to 17 knots. Within two hours the ship was close enough for Nordengen to make out the name *Sea Shepherd*. Defiantly the *Sea Shepherd* cut across the *Sierra*'s bow, then she dropped back in her wake; then again overtook the whaler and stood directly in her path. Nordengen did not know exactly who these *Sea Shepherd* people were, but he had no doubt now they were ecological protestors – and this meant trouble.

Already this year the *Sierra*'s operations had been exposed on Britain's Thames Television through a documentary by Jack Saltman. He had acted on information supplied by Nick Carter and others, and for the first time made pirate whaling front page news in Japan. Nor did the foes of the whalers limit their attack to journalism. One morning in Las Palmas harbour, when the *Sierra* started up her engines, there came a terrible grinding and meshing of steel as the engines strangled to a stop. It was soon discovered that a saboteur had wrapped a steel cable around the ship's propeller. When the engines started, the twisting cable damaged the propeller and severely twisted the shaft. The result was a three-week delay for repairs.

That was all behind them now, but who was this new gang of 'humaniacs' in this *Sea Shepherd* ship, and how had they found his ship in the open sea? Nordengen had kept his radio quiet and had given no bearings of his locations. Still, Nordengen was not rattled; he had been in many tough situations before. This was a rough business and he took to it with enthusiasm. If there were whales to be taken he would go there. In the past he had had more than his share of dangerous foes. He was not now going to be intimidated by a bunch of tree huggers.

So the chase was on: running ahead, stopping, zigzagging, running again. If the *Sea Shepherd* blocked the way, Nordengen would take a run at her, bluffing his way through against the faster ship. The chase continued through the night, running in the dark, changing course, cutting engines and lights, drifting. Then starting up again and running. Cat and mouse through the night, but Nordengen could not lose them. By dawn both ships were standing off the Portuguese coast, and by 10 a.m. they were outside the port of Leixoes.

Nordengen reasoned that as he was not whaling, the *Sea Shepherd* could not interfere with him. They would get their pictures of him while he hung about, but when the time was right would slip out and unload his cargo on to a Japanese reefer. He must avoid them then, and with the help of the port people he thought he might manage it.

At noon it looked like the *Sea Shepherd* was going to make it easy for Nordengen. It was going into port. But to Nordengen's astonishment, the *Sea Shepherd* had not been in port for more than an hour when she came storming out at full speed without a pilot and without clearance.

Then, in tactics identical to that of the sperm whale that had attacked the *Essex* over a century before, the *Sea Shepherd* cut across the bow of the *Sierra* in an attempt to sheer off the harpoon gun. The warning blow knocked the crew off their feet. The *Sea Shepherd* then swung about in a tight 360-degree turn and, charging like a mad bull whale made of steel, attempted a full-scale ramming amidship. The concrete-reinforced steel bow of the *Sea Shepherd* tore into the *Sierra* like a big axe blade, ripping the whaler open with a gash eight feet long and six feet wide, buckling in the whole side of the ship.

In the ensuing mêlée, the *Sierra* – hull torn open – fled for safety within the harbour, and the *Sea Shepherd* attempted to escape Portuguese waters. The attack had taken place in full view of port authorities, and the *Sea Shepherd* knew that action would be swiftly taken. Her bid for freedom very nearly succeeded, but eight miles from Spanish territorial waters she was overtaken by a Portuguese destroyer. Under threat of firing, the *Sea Shepherd* was escorted back to Leixoes and held captive by port authorities.

In spite of this end, the *Sea Shepherd's* avenging mission had been achieved to a degree. The outlaw whaler that had for so long eluded legal control had now herself succumbed to an outlaw action. The ramming had crippled and very nearly sunk the *Sierra*. She was laid up with several hundred thousand dollars' worth of damage, and once again she had attracted the attention of the world's press, a fame her owners were not happy to achieve.

So despite the obviously illegal ramming by the *Sea Shepherd*, the *Sierra's* infamy as a pirate whaler made it very difficult for her to find defenders. No one wanted to be publicly identified with the pirate, no matter how much it might secretly profit them.

Had Captain Nordengen known more about the *Sea Shepherd* and its captain, he might have more quickly anticipated the seriousness of their actions. The leader of the *Sea Shepherd* organization was a Canadian named Paul Watson. Although a young man, Watson was a veteran eco-guerilla. He was there in the lead Zodiacs against the Russians in that fateful first encounter when the harpoon was fired over the head of the Greenpeacers. He was a veteran of a score of campaigns from the Russian fleets in the Pacific, to the Amerindian siege at Wounded Knee, to the seal slaughters on the Newfoundland ice. He was an experienced seaman, and he was absolutely committed to saving the whales. Called a 'bull in a china shop' by Bob Hunter and '"Gentle Ben" with a sense of humour' by Cleveland Amory, Watson is a man who by turns is reckless and sensitive, amiable and quarrelsome. Vilified by his enemies, Watson's direct and uncompromising tactics even made some of his allies nervous, and many environmental groups refused to work with him. No one, however has ever doubted his courage. All sides agreed: Watson was a born kamikaze.

What had happened outside Leixoes was far from a whim; it had been thought out long ahead of time. It just required the nerve to do it, and Watson had the nerve. With the financial backing of Cleveland Amory's New York-based Fund for Animals, Watson had purchased the *Sea Shepherd*. With a large donation from the British RSPCA, he put her in shape, first to go out on the Canadian ice in the sealing season to protest the seal harvest. Then he set sail for Portugal with a vague tip as to where the *Sierra* was to be found. Against all odds, he tracked her down a few hundred miles off Portugal.

Ramming, Watson reasoned, was the only way to put the *Sierra* out of business; virtually every legal means had been tried, in vain, over the last five years. Everyone agreed the *Sierra* must go, but no one would see to it. Watson was tired of talk and cynicism.

After the ramming, Watson was surprised to find that no criminal proceedings were taken against him. His ship, however, was being held in lieu of $750,000 damages and costs claims set against her by the *Sierra*. Since the *Sea Shepherd* had been originally purchased for $120,000, Watson found this somewhat absurd.

For seven months attempts were made to gain release of the *Sea Shepherd*. However, when Watson returned to Portugal he discovered that tens of thousands of dollars' worth of equipment had been stripped from his vessel by thieves. Afraid that the ship was in danger of 'going into the hands of the enemy' by court action, Watson decided to scuttle. On New Year's Eve he and engineer Peter Woof went down into the hold, opened the sea cocks in the engine room and let the sea roar in.

3 THE BOMBERS

In early February 1980, nearly eight months since the ramming of the *Sierra* and five weeks since the scuttling of the *Sea Shepherd*, the *Sierra* was sitting quietly at rest in Lisbon harbour, refitted and tuned up after months of repairs, once again sea worthy. At exactly 6.17 in the morning there was a loud explosion as a charge tore into the *Sierra*. Into the gaping hole in her hull rushed the sea. In ten minutes, the eleven crew members watched from the dock as the *Sierra* sank to the bottom of the harbour.

When navy frogmen and maritime police completed their investigation, they concluded that a military-style magnetic limpet mine had been used. It had been set with a timing device and placed a few feet below the waterline. It had been deliberately positioned in the fore of the ship, as far as possible from the sleeping quarters. The explosive charge was large enough to hole the ship, but not large enough to injure the crew. Clearly, it had not been the work of amateurs.

After the bombing, Allan Thornton, Greenpeace's British director, said his London office was besieged by phone calls from people who wanted to help out on any new bomb raids. Some claimed commando and Vietnam war experience, others British SAS training in high explosives. The direct approach to protesting whaling seemed to strike these people as refreshingly honest. Thornton said that he had little doubt that a few of the calls were probably Interpol or British Special Branch attempting to prove Greenpeace had been involved in the bombing. However, he had the chilling feeling that several callers were genuine and frighteningly sincere in their offers to bring about an apocalyptic end to whaling.

To all, Thornton replied that he felt it would be hypocritical of him' to say he was sorry that the *Sierra* had been blown up. He was as glad as anyone to see her gone, but he was particularly disturbed that there had been people on board the ship during the bombing, for it would have been little short of a catastrophe for the Save the Whale movement if anyone had been hurt or killed. No doubt, to most of the enthusiastic callers, Thornton was a big disappointment when he said that so far as Greenpeace was concerned, non-violent direct action did not include the use of bombs.

Paul Watson, speaking for the *Sea Shepherd*, was not so quick to rule out such tactics. He was absolutely against hurting or killing any living thing, and in both the ramming and the bombing, he pointed out, no one had been injured. However, he did not feel so protective about property, particularly whaling ships.

Fortunately for Watson, he had an unsinkable alibi at the time of the explosion. He was in a Canadian courtroom surrounded by a dozen intrepid Royal Canadian Mounted Police, being tried for his part in another animal welfare crusade: the Canadian harp seal hunt. Unfortunately for Watson, he was found guilty of the sealing offences, severely fined and sent to prison.

So far as the sinking of the *Sierra* was concerned, Watson and the *Sea Shepherd* people had not in fact been involved. As Watson said, he was ignorant of exactly how the ship was blown up and by whom, until at the IWC in Brighton in 1980 he claimed to have picked up the details:

Two men and a woman went to Lisbon. While the woman stood guard, the two men 'borrowed' skiff in the harbour and rowed silently across the water to the *Sierra*, tied up in the Tagus River. All three wore wet suits, almost invisible on that dark night of 5 February 1980.

At the *Sierra*, on the side of the hull nearest the dock, the two men located the area of the refrigerator room, the large open space inside the ship where the whale meat is stored during operations. They dove some six feet below the water line and quickly attached a magnetic mine. As best they could, in the underwater darkness, they set the timing device for 6.15 the next day.

The two men swam to the surface, got back into their skiff and rowed, as silently as they had come, to another part of the docks, where the woman waited. They stripped off their wet suits, keeping out of sight under the wharves, and changed into travelling clothes. The trio then caught a taxi cab to the Lisbon railroad depot, where they boarded the midnight train to Spain.

4 THE AFRICAN PIRATES

By the time the *Sierra* was sunk there was little left in the way of sympathy for South African whaling interests. Even the outspoken Hout Bay businessman Andrew Behr who, in 1975, had cavalierly stated that 'whales are finished anyway' and that in the meantime there would be a few jobs in helping to finish them off, found he was having to change his tune. Soon after that statement, Behr was denying any connection with the *Sierra* or the *Tonna*, or any other whaling ships. He said he was 'not interested' in documents that indicated the opposite. He was similarly not interested in business cards for the Sierra Fishing Company labelled 'Division of Andrew M. Behr (Pty) Ltd', nor the fact that Sierra Fishing Company and Andrew M. Behr (Pty) Ltd shared the same letter box across the corridor from his own office.

By April 1979 Colin Eglin, the leader of the South African Opposition, was urging the government to launch an investigation into pirate whaling activities. In May Stephen Wrottesley of the

Cape Times interviewed Mr Behr, who again denied any links between the pirate whaler *Sierra* and his company. He said there was no South African company behind the *Sierra* – 'I can give you my word on that.'

At exactly this time, the Durban shipbuilders Dorman Long at Dobelmeyer yard had just made shipbuilding history by completing the biggest 'jumbo-izing' of any ships in South African history. Under a one and a half million rand contract, two old whale-catchers, renamed the *Susan* and the *Theresa*, were cut in half and had 15-metre long, 90-ton units placed in their mid-sections – thus stretching the ships to factory-size vessels. Stern slipways with refrigerator holds and freezing equipment – supplied from Japan – were installed. The ships were thus duplicates of the *Sierra*: combination killer-factory whaling ships that were outlawed by the IWC.

Behr, when questioned about these ships, claimed that they had nothing to do with him. They were not even registered in South Africa, they were registered in Panama. It was simply coincidental that the ships in question had identical names to his two daughters: Susan and Theresa.

Meanwhile, reporter Wrottesley, finding that Sierra Fishing was hiring a new crew in the Cape Town area, discovered a third ship being fitted as a whaler. This was the *M.V. Fisher*, which until very recently (he could still read the lettering beneath the new paint) was the Japanese *M.V. Yashima Maru*. Coincidentally, the *Fisher* also happened to be registered with an anonymous Panamanian company. It was obvious that the Sierra Fishing Company was expanding its fleet, and a new wave of pirate ships was about to enter the Atlantic. Nick Carter, his South African environmental colleague Nan Rice and other conservationists urged Colin Eglin to act swiftly. Pressure also came from scores of international organizations, and a government enquiry was at last launched.

The first action taken was against the *Fisher*, which in mid-May was about to leave for Las Palmas in the Canaries. Cape port authorities ordered all South African nationals off the ship. However, a skeleton crew of non-South Africans set sail for the Canaries anyway. There, the *Fisher* again underwent a change of identity and became the *Astrid*.

The *Yashima Maru/Fisher/Astrid* was meant to become another sister ship for the *Sierra*, but a few weeks later the *Sierra* was blown up in Lisbon habour. A couple of months after that, there were bomb attacks against two Spanish whalers, and shortly thereafter an agent from the *Sea Shepherd* organization appeared in the Canary Islands with reward posters offering a bounty of US $25,000 to anyone who would sink the *Astrid*. All this activity had a rather sobering effect on the ship and, finding tuna fishing less traumatic, she seems to have terminated her career as a whaler.

South African action against the *Susan* and the *Theresa* meanwhile proved more directly effective. The fitting out of the ships had been delayed in April by an extensive fire on the *Theresa*. There was some indication that this may also have been an act of sabotage, but whatever the cause, the delay was sufficient for public opinion to be roused and government action taken.

In the midst of the South African debacle, Mr Behr had the sudden urge to set up residency abroad. Whatever his reasons were for leaving, the move seems to have been long-term. Leaving behind considerable property, he found a quiet village sanctuary in Virginia Water, England, and his family soon joined him there.

The initial result of the inquiry into pirate whaling was the seizure of the *Theresa* and the *Susan* in Durban. A prolonged struggle for possession followed, which in the long run resulted in both ships being virtually sunk by the weight of red tape entangling them.

It was a victory for the conservationists. Without ever hunting a single whale, these new, record-breaking stretched whalers were being mothballed. Five years later they at last sailed the seas – as mock battle targets for the South African navy. They were shot to pieces.

5 SINKING THE SPANISH ARMADA

By means both fair and foul, the back of the Sierra Gang had been broken with the loss of the *Tonna*, the *Sierra*, the *Susan* and the *Theresa*. It was no mean victory for the conservationists. Although this most notorious gang of freelance pirates had been harried out of business, another fleet of pirate whalers in the Atlantic was still on the prowl. This was not a renegade hide-

and-seek gang of outlaws, but an official, government-sanctioned, establishment pirate who, with the full knowledge and co-operation of his government – and indeed with the backing of its navy – ruthlessly plundered the sea.

During Franco's days in Spain, one was not likely to find a sympathetic ear in government for the Save the Whale movement. One had just to look at El Caudillo's personal yacht to realize that. She had a harpoon gun mounted on her decks. Franco was a recreational whaler. He saw it as a grander form of bullfighting or big game hunting.

A survivor of the good old days with the generalissimo was Juan Jose Masso. Masso was a Galician whaler who owned Industria Ballenera SA (IBSA), Spain's only remaining whaling company, and even after Franco's demise Masso still enjoyed government support for his little Spanish Armada of whaling ships. Spain was not a member of the IWC, and this allowed Masso a free hand in his methods of whaling. As was the case with the *Sierra*, the only restrictions respected were those determined by the number of ships that could put to sea, and the state of the whale meat market.

Thanks to deals with the Japanese, the whale meat market was very good, and by 1978 Masso had four ships operating from his two Spanish whaling stations in Vigo and Cangas. In 1978 and 1979 Masso reported just under 600 whales killed each year – although conservationists found these figures suspect. Even accepting them, the IWC repeatedly requested that these numbers be drastically cut back, since they were decimating Atlantic stocks. The requests, not surprisingly, were ignored.

Acting with arrogant self-interest and backed by influence within government that allowed the defiance of international pressure, nonetheless by 1979 Masso was faced with a kind of compromise. The *Sierra* scandal and American pressure forced Japan to officially ban importation of whale meat from non-IWC countries, as of 5 July 1979. Consequently, the day before the IWC opened its meeting that summer, Spain hurriedly became a member. Thereby declared a perfectly legal whaling nation, Spain promptly shipped off its ill-gotten whale meat to Japan. With equal promptness, it wholly ignored all IWC rulings it did not wish to abide by, and continued whaling as before.

There *were* warnings. In December 1979, some five months after the ramming of the *Sierra*, two explosions were detonated near Masso's whaling ships docked in Coruna. Rather mysteriously they inflicted no damage whatever to the ships. Masso chose to ignore this incident, as he seems to have ignored the bombing of the *Sierra* a couple of months later. For him, it was business as usual.

On 27 April 1980, however, business came to an abrupt halt. Masso's ships were moored in the harbour of Marin near the Vigo whaling station in the Pontevedro estuary. Once again two explosions were heard. This time the impact blew holes in two ships, and the *Ibsa I* and the *Ibsa II* sank to the bottom of the harbour.

No one at all was aboard the ships, and no one had been harmed in the explosions. Although no one came forward to claim credit for the attack, Paul Watson said Masso's ships were 'victims of magnetic mines, one of them homemade, which had been planted by the same trio that destroyed the *Sierra*'. This, however, was a red herring. The bombers were professionals with military training and military explosives. There was nothing homemade or homespun about the bombings in either Spain or Portugal.

The bomb attacks were engineered by a man who had a deep personal commitment to saving whales. It was a commitment unhampered by the pacifist ideals embraced by most ecologists. Believing it impossible to act within any conservationist organization with any degree of security, he made no contact with any group and maintained a careful anonymity. Aware of the dangers involved, his actions were not dictated by a desire for recognition of any sort; consequently, he was personally delighted by the cover and diversion of attention provided by the *Sea Shepherd*.

Recruitment for the bomb raids was not made by acquiring the services of committed amateurs. Contact was made with a colourful and rather infamous African mercenary who went under the pseudonym 'Mr Brown'. Mr Brown had gone into semi-retirement after he had published a bizarre account of his career as a mercenary for various African regimes. However, through Mr Brown a meeting was arranged that proved to be the key to an extensive underground network of mercenaries and international arms dealers.

It was within this network that a team of professionals was found. One of the team had connections with the Portuguese military which, it was thought, would be of considerable advantage in the Iberian area, both in the acquisition and in the transportation of the explosive devices.

The first raid, however, literally misfired. In December 1979, in the Spanish port of Coruna, two men successfully fitted explosives on the hulls of the *Ibsa I* and the *Ibsa II*. Everything seemed to go perfectly, the men made a clean getaway, and early in the morning there were two sudden explosions. However, the bombs had no effect whatever on the ships, which remained defiantly buoyant and quite unharmed.

The rather shame-faced team discovered they had acquired dud explosives. However two months later they made their way across the Portuguese border and did much better on that outing. On 6 February 1980 they blew the bottom out of the *Sierra*, and in April they went back for a second shot at the Spanish fleet. This time they found the fleet in the port of Marin, and the timing of their attack was excellent. It was a Sunday and the whaling armada was to sail to the whaling grounds the following day. The crews were in the church that afternoon, seeking a blessing for a good catch. At exactly 2 p.m., while presumably awaiting some small sign of good fortune within the church, the whalers were apprised of two loud explosions in the habour.

By the time the congregation filed out of the chapel and reached the dock, all that could be seen of the *Ibsa I* and *Ibsa II* was less than 10 feet of upper mast. These marked where the whaling ships sat on the bottom of the river bed – an appropriate answer to a pirate's prayer.

After the Marin bombings, Masso's remaining ships and whaling stations were watched by armed guards night and day. Ships going into whaling grounds sailed under naval escort, as they did during the Second World War. Masso's company had become a garrison industry under constant fear of attack. It was a very uncomfortable way to run a business.

6 THE GREAT ESCAPE

On 17 June 1980, just seven weeks after the *Ibsa I* and *Ibsa II* bombings, the *Ibsa III* was once again hunting fin whales some 220 miles off the Spanish coast. There they were confronted by the now familiar ship with the rainbow-and-dove logo on her prow, the Greenpeace flagship, *Rainbow Warrior*.

The year before the same ship had successfully harassed the Masso ocean-tug the *Carrumeiro* in these same whaling grounds. As they had then, they quickly deployed their commando crews in the swift Zodiacs and began their flying picket tactics, forming a human barrier between the whales and the *Ibsa III*. For several hours these tactics were effective, but then two Spanish warships suddenly appeared. The warships did not waste time pursuing the Zodiacs, but instead headed straight for the *Rainbow Warrior*. A high-speed chase ensued. The Greenpeace activists claimed that they were in international waters, while the Spanish claimed that they were within Spain's 200-mile limit. In any event, the chase ended with a boarding by the Spanish, formal arrest of the crew and confiscation of the ship, pending trial.

It was the third time in thirteen months that the *Rainbow Warrior* had been seized by military authorities. In 1979, in the Icelandic whaling campaigns, she had had *five* harpoons fired over her Zodiacs before the Icelandic navy boarded her. In the first incident the navy seized the ship in national waters, in the second case they boarded her in international waters and illegally confiscated her Zodiacs.

This time the *Rainbow Warrior* looked like she was in even more serious trouble than before. Charged in a military court with interfering with Spanish 'fishing', she was fined $142,000 and held in the port of El Ferrol. Jonathan Castle, the *Rainbow Warrior* captain, refused to pay this fine and elected to stand trial.

With the ship placed under a 24-hour-a-day armed guard in El Ferrol, a military harbour filled with Spanish warships five miles from the open sea and beneath the guns of two forts, it seemed the Spanish navy took no chances on allowing the *Rainbow Warrior* to slip away. Furthermore, the Spanish authorities removed from the engine the 120-lb 'thrust block' – a large, essential propeller-shaft bearing without which the ship was incapable of movement.

It appeared that Juan Masso and the Spanish whalers had some measure of revenge; the *Rainbow Warrior* would either have to be abandoned or Greenpeace would be levied a crippling fine that was greater than the value of a new ship. For five months the ship gathered barnacles and seaweed. Greenpeace crewmen came and went from time to time in order to keep her seaworthy.

However, the Greenpeacers were not just idly accepting their fate. Unknown to the Spanish, a plot was hatching. Greenpeace crew members were secretly conducting an international search for a new 'thrust block'. And in time one was found, quietly purchased and smuggled into Spain in the back of a Volkswagen van. Then, in a piece of comic theatre, while singing and laughing and pretending drunkenness, the Greenpeacers lugged the 120-lb block past the guards on to the ship.

Two weeks later, just before midnight on Saturday 8 November, in the darkness of a new moon, during a change of guard, the *Rainbow Warrior* slipped from the dock and out of the port. She passed under the bows of a dozen warships and beneath the guns of two forts into the open sea five miles beyond.

All hell broke loose in El Ferrol. The naval authorities could not believe the ship had gone. How had she activated her engines? Where were the guards and gunships? Two Spanish naval frigates were immediately despatched to hunt down the Greenpeace ship and a military helicopter was sent out to spot her.

On the moonless night the ship was difficult to spot, but the *Rainbow Warrior* was considerably hampered by two factors. One was fuel. The Spanish had taken the precaution of removing most of the ship's fuel, leaving only sufficient for routine starting and maintenance of the engine. The *Rainbow Warrior* was literally running on the dregs of fuel. Secondly, the mass of barnacles and seaweed that built up over five months on her hull severely slowed her passage. So there she was fleeing on near-empty tanks, at a painful pace of six knots – half her normal speed – with the Spanish navy in hot pursuit.

Amazingly, through the skill and nerve of her captain Jon Castle, the *Rainbow Warrior* fled and eluded her pursuers that night. Then on Tuesday evening, 11 November, she sailed into the Channel Islands on dry tanks. The *Rainbow Warrior* was met in Jersey by cheering crowds of supporters. The impossible had been done, the great escape achieved.

The daring escape also resulted in one more casualty of the Whale War in the North Atlantic. Three days after the *Rainbow Warrior* sailed into Jersey, the Spanish cabinet met in an emergency session. How had a civilian environmental ship managed to escape the most heavily guarded naval base in the country? It was a terrible embarrassment to the proud Spanish military. It was clear heads must roll. The cabinet started at the top. It fired the top man at El Ferrol, Admiral Jose Maria de la Guardia y Oya. It was the end for the Spanish admiral, and, it soon emerged, the end of the Spanish pirates was also in sight.

The dramatic events of 1979–80 were the turning of the tide of the Whale War within Spain and without. Public opinion and government pressure were beginning to take their toll.

In 1981 the Spanish Socialist Workers Party (PSOE) sponsored a motion brought about by the environmental lobbies within the country that had been steadily growing since 1977. It was a binding restriction instructing the Spanish IWC delegates to vote for a moratorium and immediate cessation of all whaling. On 16 December 1981, the vote was taken. It was passed with an overwhelming majority, signalling parliament's complete turn-about.

7 PIRATE GRAVEYARD

Since the ill omen of the sinking of the *Tonna* by a whale in 1978, the luck of the pirate whalers in the Atlantic, it would seem, just ran out. In the fierce blitzkrieg between 16 July 1979, when the *Sierra* was rammed by the *Sea Shepherd*, and 17 June 1980, when the *Rainbow Warrior* was seized, there had been extraordinary acts of 'ecotage', the likes of which the environmental movement had never before seen. There had been four bomb explosions in Spain and one in Portugal, resulting in the sinking of three ships. Another ship in Portugal had been scuttled, there was a shipboard fire in South Africa, several high-speed gunboat chases, ship-boardings and seizures, and numerous lesser acts of sabotage. The actions of that period led to further incidents, such as the eventual demolition and sinking of two South African whaling ships, the daring night escape of the *Rainbow Warrior*, the firing of the Spanish admiral and the turnabout of the Spanish parliament.

It was trial by fire in the Atlantic theatre of the Whale War, and the pirate whalers were driven out. The Atlantic had become a pirate whalers' graveyard. Six pirate ships had sunk and three others been forced into premature retirement, whereas the environmentalists had lost only one ship. No time for complacency, for they knew the enemy would not let up, but now nine less ships hunted whales in the Atlantic.

In the midst of the debacle in the Atlantic theatre of war, there was a rather fascinating sideshow, a sub-plot to the *Sierra* drama. In the time between the ramming of the *Sierra* and her eventual sinking, the ever-resourceful French ecologist Jean-Paul Fortom-Gouin appeared in Portugal with the most unlikely convert to the Save the Whale movement in its history. It was perhaps the strangest alliance of personalities in the entire conflict: the little French ecologist and the huge six-and-a-half-foot Norwegian, Captain Knud Hansen. Unbelievably, Hansen was the inventor of the combination killer-factory ship, the creator of the *Sierra*, the prototype pirate whaler. He was a captain-gunner who by his own hand had killed 17,000 whales, more than any man alive.

Captain Hansen now claimed to have had a sudden change of heart and wished to offer his services in the cause of the ecologists. Not wishing to appear incredulous at the ex-pirate captain's born-again vision of a peaceful world for whales, the ecologists asked cautiously what he had in mind.

Hansen had a proposition. He told the ecologists how he had lost the *Sierra* in what he alleged was a double-cross and fraudulent bankruptcy. For a time after that he ran another ship, carrying dubious cargoes before and during the Angolan war, then he attempted building up some new business. But once again he had fallen on hard times, and in this altered financial condition came to meditate on his past deeds. When he came to think of the *Sierra*, it was then he suddenly saw the error of his ways. In short, for a certain cash incentive, he was now willing to see the moral rightness of the Save the Whale movement.

The proposal, then, was simple. If the ecologists would finance his attempt to get his ship back from the courts, he would champion their cause. He would use the *Sierra* to fight the whalers. He would just take her out and ram and sink other whaling ships!

The enthusiasm of this convert made a few conservationists more than a little nervous. Most believed his motives were transparently financial and in any case were not enthusiastic at the idea of giving Hansen his ship back. Half thought he might easily double-cross them and go whaling, and the other half thought the consequences might even be worse if he kept his word. Only Jean-Paul Fortom-Gouin thought such an ally might be worthwhile. So, in a scene reminiscent of Dr Frankenstein's attempt to reclaim his monster, the Frenchman and the Norwegian flew into Portugal and went to the courts and port authorities to legally seize the *Sierra* on Hansen's behalf. The attempted seizure, unfortunately, failed after three months, and others had to come up with a final solution for the *Sierra*.

Never missing an opportunity, Hansen then suggested to the conservationists that, as the *Sierra* deal did not work out, perhaps for a moderate fee they might like to hire his other ship to terrorize the whalers? Perhaps, he suggested, it took a pirate to stop a pirate. Somehow no environmental group could bring itself to trust anyone who had personally killed 17,000 whales. Sadly, his offer was graciously declined.

The dubious conversion of Captain Knud Hansen was not the only remarkable desertion from the *Sierra*'s crew. With considerably less to gain than Hansen, another of the *Sierra*'s crew, its first mate and harpooner Knut Hustredt appeared in 1981 on the NBC TV programme 'Amazing Animals'. This programme reviewed the more spectacular events in the Whale War, such as the ramming and the sinking of the *Sierra*.

It was a retrospective of the extreme tactics used by some environmental activists. Curiously, the harpooner did not seem to hold a grudge. He even pointed out that the men who stood against the *Sierra* had themselves risked their lives. Before the ramming of the *Sierra*, he had never really thought much about the killing. It was then almost inconceivable to him that someone would risk his life to save a whale. Now he saw things differently.

But what of the tactics used against the *Sierra* – surely they were dangerous and ill-considered?

The harpooner shrugged. 'It was the only way we could have been stopped.'

PART THREE

'The strength of the Save the Whale movement is in its diversity.'

CRAIG VAN NOTE *Monitor*

6

RAIDING THE RUSSIANS

1 INVASION OF SIBERIA

Much to the surprise of the Americans, not to mention the Russians, the Soviet Union was invaded by foreign troops on 9 August 1981. True, the invasion did not bring about the collapse of the nation's defence system, nor did it result in the toppling of the government. In fact, it was a very small-scale invasion. An enemy warship entered Russian waters and landed commandos on a beach before they were confronted by soldiers, warships and helicopter gunships.

What was this all about? The strategic high command may have been confused, but the Soviet whaling commissioner had a reasonable idea.

The reason for all this dramatic activity was an obscure item in the IWC quota system that had for some years puzzled conservationists. This item allowed the USSR each year to take, in a non-commercial hunt, some 200 otherwise protected California grey whales from their shallow Bering Sea feeding grounds off the Chukchi peninsula in Siberia.

This subsistence aboriginal hunt was not like the American Eskimo hunt carried out by native people themselves. The Soviets argued that in order to make the hunt more efficient, it was carried out on behalf of the aboriginal people by a single modern catcher boat called the *Zevezdny*.

What was puzzling to ecologists was the fact that until 1955

73

the aboriginal catch varied from as little as 10 to 30 whales a year, but after 1955 it rose to nearly 200 a year and remained there. Conservationists estimated that the average aboriginal family on the Chukchi peninsula, to use up the whales killed, would be required to consume something like *10 tons* of whale meat per year – a rather daunting task.

So where, conservationists wanted to know, were the whales going? No information was forthcoming. The Russians, for unspecified security reasons, would allow no observers to see either the hunt or the native villages the whales were being delivered to.

This, then, was the reason for the invasion of Siberia. The warship that launched the invasion was the *Sea Shepherd II*, the second incarnation of the ship that under the command of Paul Watson had been the scourge of the Atlantic pirates. It was now the same Paul Watson who led this new crew of eco-guerillas.

From Nome, Alaska, Watson sailed across the Bering Strait and on 9 August entered Soviet waters. The *Sea Shepherd II* was met almost immediately not by Soviet ships but by hundreds of grey whales in their feeding grounds, swarming about the ship. Sailing down the Siberian coast, by mid-day Watson reached the Soviet whaling station village of Loren. Leaving the *Sea Shepherd II* standing two miles offshore, Watson and two crew members leapt into their commando Zodiac and sped towards the beach.

Watson retells the incident:

We landed about a hundred feet from the whaling station. Piles of fresh whale meat littered the area with some very un-aboriginal-type women employed with hacking the hunks of meat into smaller pieces with some mean-looking flensing knives. We were close enough to see their blondish hair tied back with bandanas and to notice that some of them had blue eyes. So much for the aboriginal justification for the hunt. The amazing part was that the women seemed completely unconcerned with our presence.

They went about their business seemingly oblivious to us. We watched as they tossed the smaller pieces of the whale meat on to a conveyor belt. The meat was transported up the slope to a small warehouse on the bluff overlooking the beach. This warehouse was bordered by the sheds that we had seen from the ship.

These sheds were long and narrow, and we counted more than fifty of them. We could plainly see that the sheds were shelters for what were obviously cages. The number of sheds could easily accommodate tens of thousands of small captives. . .

We were looking at a mink ranch! Our suspicions had been justified. This so-called aboriginal hunt was nothing more than a front for a commercial mink farm. The whales were simply a cheap source of fodder for a lucrative fur business.

Watson's observations and filming of the scene were soon interrupted by two Soviet soldiers armed with rifles. As Watson was later to conclude, both the soldiers and the women must have assumed Watson and his team were Russian scientists or industrial management people whom they had not been informed were visiting. However, when the ecologists at last spoke in a language that was not Russian, the error was suddenly realized. The astonished soldiers quickly unslung their rifles, but did not fire as the conservationists leapt back into their Zodiac and fled to their ship.

Immediately after Watson boarded the *Sea Shepherd II*, he found himself pursued by two Soviet army helicopter gunships and a 300-foot Soviet destroyer. The helicopter gunships fired flares across the bow and on to the decks of the *Sea Shepherd II*. The Soviet destroyer attempted to stop the Greenpeace ship, threatening to fire on her and trying to block her progress. At one point the *Sea Shepherd II* nearly repeated her namesake's performance and came close to ramming the destroyer rather than permitting a boarding.

The Soviets had found themselves caught off-guard, and they. must have thought they were dealing with crazy people. Watson refused to obey radio and signal commands to stop, and in the midst of the pursuit he gave the Soviet commander a lecture on the immorality of whaling over the radio. The chase lunged on, but after four hours the Soviet destroyer had not fired her guns, and as the *Sea Shepherd II* re-entered the safe refuge of American waters, the destroyer and the helicopters withdrew.

2 BACK IN THE USSR

Not to be outdone by its old rival the *Sea Shepherd*, and in the face of the Soviet refusal to confirm or deny that whales were killed primarily to feed mink, Greenpeace decided a second invasion of Russia was on the cards. With their typically acute sense of timing, Greenpeace set the invasion in motion right in the midst of the July 1983 IWC conference week, to take advantage of the press attention to whaling.

Attract attention they certainly did. The *Rainbow Warrior*, like the *Sea Shepherd II* before her, made for the grey whale feeding grounds in the Bering Sea and on 18 July landed her invasion force of six men and women on the Siberian beach at the whaling station of Loren. Once again the puzzled inhabitants of Loren faced an ecology warship sitting offshore, while Zodiacs buzzed their beaches and strangers stood on the shore.

But this time the Soviets were better prepared than they had been two years before. Soldiers and police closed in and seized those on the beaches. Helicopters descended, pursuing the cameramen in the Zodiacs who were photographing and filming the station and arrests. One helicopter gunship plucked a cameraman right out of his running Zodiac. However, at the price of a broken ankle, the television film and photographs were rescued by one brave Greenpeace crewman who leapt from the deck of the *Rainbow Warrior* into the runaway Zodiac as it passed the ship.

Immediately after, the helicopters and gunboats closed in on the *Rainbow Warrior* herself. Running her engines full-speed, the *Rainbow Warrior* raced towards American waters. The helicopters fired flares and the warships, joined by other Soviet vessels, pursued. The Soviet warship demanded surrender as she and a freighter attempted to block the *Warrior*'s passage and fence her in between the ships. Greenpeace captain Peter Wilcox cut his engines, but then rapidly accelerated again, outmanoeuvring the Soviet ships. The chase lasted more than six hours, but at last the Greenpeacers reached the safety of American waters, and eventual anchorage in Nome.

Meanwhile, back on the beach in army custody, were seven eco-guerillas, but, after holding the ecologists for a few days in a military barrack, the Russians decided these people were after all not a high-priority espionage risk. Five days later, two Soviet warships and three other Soviet vessels arranged a peaceful rendezvous with the *Rainbow Warrior* on the Alaskan-Russian border in the Bering Strait. Here, the mayor of Nome Leo Rasmussen, crossed between the ships in a Greenpeace Zodiac and collected the seven Greenpeace invaders from the Soviets. In return, Rasmussen shook the Soviets' hands and gave the Soviets an 'I Love Nome' button.

In the end the grey whale 'aboriginal hunt' got its publicity, and there were repercussions in the IWC meetings, but not many. The Soviet commission still refused any information, despite Greenpeace's photographic evidence and testimonies. Reluctantly, however, the Soviet commissioner said that at long last there was now being compiled a research study on the aboriginal population's nutritional and cultural need for the grey whale harvest, which would be presented to the IWC – in some future year.

Unable to contain its cynicism towards the Soviet position, the official publication of the IWC non-governmental organizations, *ECO*, published what it purported to be a leaked draft of an early report on the 'nutritional and cultural aboriginal needs' that the grey whale hunt fulfilled, as laid down by IWC regulations.

Nutritional needs: local aboriginals have been heavily reliant on whale meat for many, many generations, back to 1956. Whale meat supplies their principal food source, as locked cage doors prevent their seeking out a more varied diet.

Cultural needs: long-term definitive study has shown that the local inhabitants have important, but little understood, feeding rituals. Active pacing begins shortly before feeding time, and cultural leaders are sometimes seen to climb on top of watering dishes in expectation of whale dinners.

Hunt by aboriginals: though now a lost tradition, is said to have been one of the phenomenal spectacles of nature. Thousands of individuals, in a highly disciplined and carefully timed manoeuvre, would swim out into the water, encircle the whale, sink their needle-sharp teeth into its hide and tow it ashore. . . .

ECO will provide more sections of the report as they are received. . . .

Indeed.

7

THE PACIFIC PIRATES

1 CHILEAN OUTLAW

I was sound asleep when they first knocked on my door. I was hoping it was actually across the hall and would go away. The sound was louder the second time, and I distinctly heard incomprehensible male voices beckoning me. Stumbling out of bed, I partially dressed and unlocked the door.

Four Chilean men walked into my room and asked if they could talk to me for a while. They said they were from Interpol. Did I understand? One man in sunglasses motioned me to a chair while another took my passport to compare me and my photo to a composite drawing on a wanted poster. Another man pulled out a notebook and began to write down everything that was said.

They wanted to know exactly why I had come to Chile, what I had done since I arrived, and who did I know in their country? I answered as best I could in my broken Spanish, and a thorough search of my bags followed. They insisted on listening to two particular cassettes so I played them 'Moonlight Sonata' and twenty minutes of blank tape.

What had I taken pictures of? I described the seabirds around San Vincente with great enthusiasm. A few minutes later, the man in sunglasses apologized profusely when he 'accidentally' opened the back of my camera, exposing a roll of film. I barely managed to recover my address book one agent had 'absentmindedly' slipped into his pocket. They left after about an hour and a half without ever telling me why they had come.

This is Greenpeace agent Campbell Plowden's account of a midnight visit by a squad of the dreaded DINA, the Chilean junta's secret police who were responsible for many thousands of 'disappearances'. Plowden had aroused their interest by snooping around the Macaya Brothers whaling operations in San Vincente. Fortunately for Plowden, the DINA agents narrowly missed finding the film and notes that would have incriminated him. Nonetheless, Plowden took the wisest course and fled the country.

Plowden's visit was in January 1979. Later, in April 1981, a second Greenpeace agent, Paul Bruce, made another secret visit. Bruce came back with more photographic evidence, and this was to be supplemented by a third agent's photographs in June of the same year.

What had drawn the Greenpeace agents to penetrate the very tight Chilean security was that nation's illegal whaling operations. For two decades Chile had been one of Japan's South American whaling colonies. However, because of the deteriorated state of the Macaya Brothers fleet of three outdated coastal whalers the damage it could do was limited. Indeed, by 1976 its performance was so poor it managed to kill only 77 whales in a year.

However, ecological investigations in 1978 revealed that this dying pirate industry suddenly and unaccountably was slaughtering over 500 whales a year. What the Greenpeace agents' investigations revealed was that through Japanese investment, the Macaya Brothers had acquired a new, and highly illegal, killer-factory ship, the *Juan 9*. Although in 1979 Chile had attempted to go legal by joining the IWC, it led the commission to believe it ran only a coastal operation. However, the *Juan 9* was a deep sea factory ship, hunting year-round, killing protected species and taking as much as five times its allotted quota. In short, it was a pirate operation.

Further undercover work revealed that the *Juan 9* was previously called *Paulmy Star III*, and before that the *Orient Maru No. 2* of Japan. Since it was illegal to export whalers to non-IWC nations from Japan, export documents stated: 'The purpose of such procurement is its use for shrimp trawling off the coast of Panama.' But the ship never came within 3,000 miles of

Panama and was equipped with a stern slipway and a harpoon gun.

Strange to say, but to the inexperienced eyes of most conservationists, there is something incongruous in stalking the treacherous and wily shrimp with a 160-lb exploding harpoon. So much so that one observer at the IWC felt compelled to remark to the commission that in his admittedly slight experience: 'A harpoon gun is not famous as a productive weapon against shrimp.'

From 1981 to 1983, Chilean authorities claimed to be investigating accusations of illegal activity, but came to no satisfactory conclusions. US diplomatic pressure and IWC censure did have some restraining effect on the number of whales killed, yet the operation continued.

There were other plans afoot by environmentalists involving confrontation and sabotage, but the iron hand of the Chilean junta made such actions hazardous in the extreme. Finally, it seems, it took a trick of fate to bring real change.

In 1984, in unexplained circumstances, the *Juan 9* broke her propeller shaft. Unable to hunt, she fell into serious financial trouble. In 1985 she was seized by creditors.

2 THE BOYS FROM PERU

In relation to whales, the Japanese have the fame of Attila the Hun, and granting them exclusive licence to hunt whales in our seas in 1970 was a bit like making Dracula a nurse maid.
Caretas, Peru's national magazine,
March 1978

Pirate whaling operations were as widespread in the Pacific as they were in the Atlantic. The lucrative black market for whale meat in Japan had opened the door to freebooters the world over. In the Pacific eco-detectives tracked down no less than five major illegal operations in Chile, Peru, Taiwan, South Korea and the Philippines.

Since the 1960s the Japanese have controlled whaling in South America. In order to avoid IWC quotas and restrictions on hunting endangered species, they have opened nominally national operations in Brazil on the Atlantic and Peru and Chile on the Pacific.

Brazil became an IWC member in 1974, but Peru and Chile remained pirate whalers until American threats of trade sanctions forced them to join in 1979. However, joining the IWC did nothing to mend the ways of these nations, and they continued to act as pirates, violating all regulations and quotas visited upon them. Indeed, Peru has only bothered to pay its nominal membership fees once in seven years of IWC membership.

Peru's Japanese-managed and -controlled Victoria Del Mar Company (Vicmar) operated three coastal whalers, the *Victoria 1, 2* and *7*, and remained very much a pirate operation within the IWC.

In December 1982, to protest against Peru's continued violations, in Greenpeace flagship, the *Rainbow Warrior*, entered Peruvian waters. On 13 December, seven Greenpeace crew members boarded the *Victoria 7* at Paita and chained themselves to the harpoon gun. For a day and a night they immobilized operations. At 3 a.m. Peruvian marines armed with machine guns arrived aboard. Using cutting torches, the marines severed the chains and placed the activists under arrest.

When the public prosecutor considered the charge of piracy against the Greenpeace activists, many Peruvians protested on their behalf. Such a charge carried a prison term of three to 20 years. Felipe Benavides, Peru's leading ecologist, stated that 'the Japanese are the only true pirates who are robbing Peru of its last few whales'.

After three days the Greenpeace activists were released with a $3,000 fine, and after two weeks the *Rainbow Warrior* was also released.

The following year saw a continued American diplomatic and economic assault on Peruvian whaling activities and threats of trade sanctions because of repeated violations and objections. However despite its continued truancies and reluctance to admit defeat, it seems Peru was finally forced to commit itself to ending its whaling operations in 1986.

3 PIRATES OF THE SOUTH CHINA SEA

In 1978 conservationists first became aware of a pirate whaling operation being run from the Taiwanese port of Kaohsiung when a ship called the *Sea Bird* was photographed unloading whale meat. By 1979 they found that a total of four pirate vessels were running a large-scale operation involving thousands of tons of whale meat.

In late 1979 and early 1980 Campbell Plowden and four other Greenpeace agents began investigations in Taiwan. This was the same Campbell Plowden who earlier in the year was interrogated by Chilean DINA agents and who later in Peru would be among those who chained themselves to the *Victoria 7* whaler, and were placed under arrest.

Plowden, a tall, slim man with a disarming boyish and open manner, has proved a tough and innovative activist and has become one of Greenpeace's most effective field agents in the Pacific theatre. Stationed in Japan, he would soon uncover numerous violations by Japanese whalers at their coastal whaling operations. Meanwhile, his contacts in Japan helped ensure maximum publicity for exposing the Taiwanese operation within that country.

At the beginning of the Greenpeace team's probe into the operation, Taiwanese officials were denying the existence of a whaling fleet, and Japan denied that it had ever imported Taiwanese whale meat. Investigations soon revealed that the four ships (*Sea Bird, Sea Flower, Chu Feng* and *Chi Hsin*) were originally Japanese ships, having gone through three name changes and dummy Panamanian ownership. The ships were currently Japanese-controlled and financed. They were also largely run with Japanese nationals in key crew positions.

Greenpeace could prove that thousands of tons of pirate whale meat were being shipped out of Taiwan, but somehow none of it was shown on Japanese import statistics to have reached Japan, the only possible market.

To unravel the Taiwanese mystery, Greenpeace agents Campbell Plowden and Rebecca Clark went to the other end of the whale meat pipeline: the huge Tokyo fish and whale meat markets. At a stall of the Shokuryo Kabushiki Gaisha in Tsukiji market, they found a box marked 'Quick Frozen Whale Meat – Whale Products – Packed by Marine Enterprise Co., Ltd., Seoul, Korea – Product of Korea.' Campbell Plowden knew from his research that Korea only exported to Japan fresh whale meat packed in ice.

Plowden and Clark decided to buy the meat. When Plowden casually mentioned that he thought Korea only sent fresh meat to Japan, the market manager candidly volunteered what was an open secret in the market: the meat was actually Taiwanese and had come via Korea. A rapid look at Korean whale meat statistics revealed the astonishing fact that although Japan recorded importing 1,800 tons of whale meat from Korea in 1979, the Koreans themselves only recorded the export of 400 tons. It was suddenly and blatantly obvious that the Taiwanese had set up a Korean whale meat laundering operation.

To further document their case, Plowden and Clark went to South Korea and the Marine Enterprises dockside processing plant, where they gathered testimonies and proof that a further 1,000 tons of Taiwanese whale meat was to be 'repacked' with Korean labels and shipped to Japan.

Late in February 1980 Plowden and Clark took their documents to Washington DC to present evidence to the Departments of State and Commerce investigations of pirate whaling operations. Within days Japanese customs agents, operating on an anonymous tip, seized 300 tons of 'Korean' whale meat, on the grounds that it had been fraudulently labelled and illegally imported from Taiwan.

By September it was clearly impossible for Taiwan to deny the existence of its whaling fleet or to justify the illegal factory pirate vessels prohibited by the IWC. It was also clear that the US fully intended to put into place trade sanctions and exclude Taiwanese fishermen from American waters. Furthermore, Japan was trying to distance itself as much as possible from the operation, and, far from admitting implication in it, swore it would seize any further importation of Taiwanese whale meat.

Taiwan performed an act of rapid surgery. Amputation was the only way to save the patient. The government seized all four pirate whaling ships and impounded their harpoons and whaling equipment. By the end of September 1980 pirate whaling in Taiwan was no more.

4 PHILIPPINE SWITCH

For a time it seemed there was a lull in the pirate whaling of the South China Sea. When the Philippines joined the IWC in 1981 the move was greeted with some enthusiasm by ecologists because the Philippines was avowedly a conservationist nation. However, the Philippines proved to be a wolf in sheep's clothing.

Soon after it joined the IWC, a Japanese businessman appeared on the scene and set up a whaling company; in May 1983 the Philippines unilaterally announced that it would kill 200 Bryde's whales.

The new company was not content with running a simple, legal, shore-based whaling operation. Once again investigations revealed that a former Japanese ship had been converted into an illegal killer-factory ship. The *Faith 1* was a duplicate of the *Sierra* prototype pirate whaler.

When this pirate ship was exposed at the 1983 and 1984 IWC meetings, the Philippines commission made a series of truly ludicrous defences of their whaling operation. They convinced no one. However, the IWC was the least of the Philippine whalers' problems. They had far more dangerous opponents: the Japanese whalers themselves.

The Philippine operation made a fatal primary error. The waters it chose to exploit were already being hunted by established Japanese coastal whalers backed by the big Japanese fishing companies. The Japanese government acted with stunning speed to protect its 'own' whales. It immediately passed a whole battery of legislation that until now it had claimed was impossible to institute against other pirate operations (obviously because they were secretly profiting from other pirate operations, whereas the *Faith 1* was cutting directly into the interests of Japan's local whalers). The result was the immediate withdrawal of Japanese investment, expertise and Japanese crew members. It also banned import of Philippine whale meat.

Overnight the Japanese forced the Philippine operation to accept a reduced quota of 55 whales and to agree to take an IWC inspector on board to make sure coastal whaling regulations were followed. However, without Japanese whaling expertise, the *Faith 1* failed even to fill its reduced quota. In 1985 it was in severe financial trouble and failing to fill its contract obligations, and it appeared as if the whaling industry in the Philippines was to end before it could even properly begin.

In Peru, Chile, Taiwan, Korea and the Philippines, pirate or illegal operations have been confronted by determined ecological activists and agents. As with the Atlantic blitz, major victories have been achieved. Although these victories should be celebrated, they are not a cause for complacency. Over the past five years, unexplained sightings of what are believed to be whaling ships have been reported in waters off Tenerife, Hawaii, the Windward Islands, Indonesia, Ireland and the Azores. Suspicions of illegal operations are also aroused in the waters off the Netherlands, Antilles, Guinea and southern Chile. Conservationists realize they must keep a constant vigil. So long as large profits can be made on the Japanese market, the pirates will try their luck.

Chile	Peru
1978 • Macaya Bros. fleet of 3 outdated coastal whalers, *Indus 17, 18,* and *19* in unregulated pirate operation. Sell meat in Japan • Evidence of sudden increase of pirate whaling (1976–77 whales killed – soars to over 500 annually). This linked to new Japanese investment and illegal import of Japanese-Panama registered factory ship *Paulmy Star III*	**1978** • *Vicmar* (Victoria del Mar Co.) operate three pirate coastal whalers *Victoria 1, 2, 7.* Registered with dummy Panama company, but Japanese owned and managed since 1967 • Evidence of killing of blue whales and other protected whales, also undersized whales. Numerous other violations. IWC protests ignored
1979 • Chile joins IWC under threat of US sanctions and Japanese ban on pirate meat • Greenpeace agent Plowden investigates	**1979** • Peru joins IWC under threat of US sanctions and Japanese ban on pirate meat • Immediately violates quota of 400 by taking 600 through a 'misunderstanding'
1980 • Publicly agrees to IWC quotas, but secretly violates both quotas and regulations	**1980** • Fails to submit to IWC quotas or regulations – or even to pay membership fees
1981 • 2nd Greenpeace agent photographs illegal factory ship *Juan 9* (once *Paulmy Star III*). Discovers she hunts year round, kills protected species, and as much as 5 times her quota • 3rd Greenpeace agent confirms *Juan 9* evidence	**1981** • Further violations – fails to submit to IWC quotas or regulations – non-payment of fees
1982 • Chilean commission of IWC claims to be investigating violations. No report is ever made. Factory ship violations continue	**1982** • IWC files objection to moratorium • *Rainbow Warrior* action in Peru. Crew chain themselves to harpoon of *Victoria 7*
1983 • Violations continue	**1983** • Violations continue

Figure 7.1 The Pacific campaign 1978–85

Chile	Peru
1984 • *Juan 9* breaks propeller shaft. In serious financial trouble	**1984** • Peru withdraws objection to IWC moratorium under US pressure • Ignores quota of 165 by taking 220. (Not once has it abided by quotas — and only once has it paid IWC fees.) Other violations continue
1985 • *Juan 9* seized by creditors • 0 quota	**1985** • Peru fails to even attend IWC • 0 quota

Russia	
1978 • Two Russian pelagic fleets reduced to one • Sperm whale violations suspected but not proved	**1982** • IWC moratorium vote passes 25–7 (3-year phase out of commercial whaling). Russia files objection, consequently refuses to abide by decision
1979 • Pelagic whaling ban at IWC for all except minke whales • Soviet fleet immediately kills 331 sperm whales in violation of ban. Explains this was unintentional and due to a 'misunderstanding'	**1983** • *Rainbow Warrior* invades Siberia 18 July – lands at Loren to protest against grey whale kill. 7 crew captured, but ship escapes. Prisoners later returned
1980 • Russians kill 1,000 orcas to supplement their quota. IWC moves to ban killing of orcas	**1984** • Russia exceeds minke whale IWC quota by 1,086
1981 • *Sea Shepherd* invades Siberia, 9 August – lands at whaling station at Loren to protest against grey whale kill. Pursued sea and air	**1985** • April – Soviets certified under Pelly Amendment and suffer fishing rights sanctions in US waters equivalent to $10 million • July – IWC will set own quotas for 1986, but Soviets announce end to whaling 1987

Figure 7.1 cont.

87

Taiwan	Korea
1978 • Dr Roger Payne photographs *Sea Bird*. First evidence of Taiwanese pirates that began operations in 1976. Joined by 2nd pirate factory ship *Sea Flower* in 1977	**1978** • Korea's 20 part-time coastal whalers sharply increase unregulated hunting as Japanese IWC quotas fall. Large exports to Japan • [December] Korea reluctantly joins IWC because of impending US legislation which forces Japan to ban non-IWC meat import
1979 • July – 3rd pirate ship *Chu Feng* appears • August – Taiwan denies existence of fleet of whalers. Declares no whale meat export • September – 4th pirate ship *Chi Hsin* joins fleet • December – Greenpeace agents in Taiwan	**1979** • Korean 'laundry' for importation of illegal Taiwanese whale meat into Japan set up • Korea's 1st IWC – quotas and restrictions agreed at prove to be immediately violated
1980 • January – Greenpeace agents discover Korean 'laundry' operation. Follows pipeline from Taiwan to Korea to Japan • February – Japanese press breaks pirate scandal • February – Greenpeace presents evidence of Taiwanese pirates in Washington. Sanctions threat • April – Japanese seize Taiwanese meat at customs • September – Taiwanese pirate whaling ends. Taiwan government forced to seize all 4 pirate ships and impound whaling equipment	**1980** • January – Greenpeace agents investigate whale meat 'laundry' – Marine Enterprises Co., Seoul • Korean 'laundry' operation is closed down • Korean coastal whalers kill protected fin and right whales, by reporting them as Bryde's whales

Figure 7.1 cont.

Philippines	Korea
1981 • Philippines joins IWC as conservationist nation	**1981** • IWC Scientific Committee proves that Korean 'Bryde's' whales are in fact illegally caught fin whales (only four real Bryde's whales found in Korean waters in last 50 years)
1982 • Philippines abstains on moratorium vote	
	1982 • Korean IWC delegation promises strict control of kill. But no observer sent
1983 • Philippines switches to a whaling nation • Conservationists reveal *Faith 1* is illegal factory ship backed by Japaness businessman Masashi Kubota	**1983** • Fin whales continue to be killed illegally
1984 • Conflict arises with Japanese whalers who claim same waters as their own • April – Japanese ban Philippine meat import • Japanese force Philippines to reduce quota from 200 to 55. But as Japanese investment and covers withdrawn from *Faith 1*, she fails to even meet reduced quota	**1984** • Fin and some right whales continue to be killed illegally
1985 • *Faith 1* unable to meet contract quotas. Serious financial trouble • 0 quota for 1986 (IWC moratorium)	**1985** • Korea uses IWC loophole in ruse to continue whaling. Issues itself a 'scientific permit' to kill 200 whales a year

Figure 7.1 cont.

Plate 1 The Russian front: Greenpeace Zodiac raiders in pursuit of the Vostok fleet, the first pelagic whaling fleet to be confronted by protesters on the high seas

Plate 2 The kamikazes: Paul Watson (centre) with Peter Woof (left) and Jerry Doran on board the *Sea Shepherd* shortly after they rammed the *Sierra*

Plate 3 Spanish showdown: a Spanish navy frigate swoops in to seize the *Rainbow Warrior* in order to stop Zodiac actions against the *Ibsa III* in whaling grounds

Plate 4 Pirate graveyard: the Spanish whaler *Ibsa II* shortly after she was bombed in the port of Marin

Plate 5 Pirate graveyard: the wreck of the notorious *Sierra* three years after rough justice ended her pirate career in Lisbon harbour

Plate 6 The Samurai: the front line of the 30-strong Japanese delegation at the International Whaling Commission in Brighton. Commissioner Yonezawa is second on the left

Plate 7 The Soviets: Dr I. V. Nikonorov (centre) surprised many by surviving as head of the IWC delegation after he was implicated in a multi-million dollar black market caviar scandal. His immediate boss, Vladimur Rytov, was executed by firing squad in 1982 over the affair

Plate 8 The vigil: Save the Whale demonstrators outside the Metropole Hotel in Brighton awaiting the outcome of the critical 1982 IWC moratorium vote. On the far right, in front of the barrier, is Sir Peter Scott of the World Wildlife Fund

Plate 9 Victory: the lobby of the Metropole Hotel moments after the IWC moratorium on whaling has been won. Jean-Paul Fortom-Gouin shares his champagne with Greenpeace International director David McTaggert

Plate 12 *Rainbow Warrior*: Greenpeace's flagship the morning after the blast that sank her in Auckland harbour

Plate 13 The explosion on the *Rainbow Warrior* resulted in the death of crew member and photographer Fernando Pereira

Plate 14 Greenpeace-UK director Allan Thornton who acquired the *Rainbow Warrior* for the organization in 1978

Plate 10 Peruvian pirate: Campbell Plowden chains himself to the harpoon gun of the *Victoria 7*

Plate 11 Peruvian pirate: conservationist Felipe Benevides examines the pirate's handiwork in the form of a dead blue whale on a Peruvian beach. Supposedly protected worldwide for over 20 years, this blue whale is just one of many illegally slaughtered each year by pirate operations

Plate 15 War zone: one Iceland's *Hvalur* ships firing a harpoon into the back of a whale in the North Atlantic

Plate 16 War zone: the Japanese whaler *Ryuho Maru #10* in the North Pacific brings in a sperm whale for butchering. Both nations continue whaling today in violation of all treaty rulings

All photographs courtesy of Greenpeace, except Plate 2 which is courtesy of Sea Shepherd/Marcus Halevi

PART FOUR

'Whales should be saved for the future, not as meat balls, but truly for the long future of mankind; for their symbolic value for man and for our environment.'

COMMISSIONER SINGH
WC Indian Delegate

8

PEACE OFFENSIVE

1 NEW INITIATIVES

The year 1982 was a special year in the Whale War, and everyone involved knew it. Two days before the annual IWC conference in Brighton in July, the Friends of the Earth launched the Last Whale Rally in London's Hyde Park which was attended by nearly 20,000 people. According to FOE organizer Charles Secrett, it was the largest animal rights rally ever and was a confident assertion in the belief that the long-awaited moratorium on commercial whaling would be won that year.

This D-Day in the Whale War did not spontaneously happen any more than the Normandy invasion just happened. Its genesis was in that most critical year of the Whale War, 1979.

That year was the beginning of the Atlantic front line blitz which eventually brought the *Sierra*, *Ibsa I*, *Ibsa II*, *Susan* and *Theresa* to rough justice and watery graves. The frustration with the IWC's inability to control the whalers, the duplicity of Japan, the betrayal of the US and the pirate epidemic also led to radical new diplomatic offensives both inside and outside the IWC.

Inside the IWC, 1979 saw the conservationists infiltrate the commission's primary defence system: its Scientific Committee. For years the IWC whaling nations had defended their position as 'scientifically based harvesting'.

In 1979 the People's Trust for Endangered Species financed scientists Dr Richard Beddington and Dr Justin Cooke to create population studies for whale species. Other research was gathered and analysed by Dr Sidney Holt and Dr William de la Mare. When these scientists reviewed the research on which IWC quotas were based and compared it to their own independent research, they were appalled and often outraged. The raw data in many cases was virtually non-existent – and often where it did exist it was highly suspect. Many nations resisted gathering any data at all; others intentionally withheld data that proved detrimental to gaining high quotas. Other times the most basic errors in biology and population dynamics were passed over.

The infiltration of the IWC Scientific Committee by scientists *not* dependent on the whaling industry itself for employment was a major breakthrough in the war. The 'science' of the whalers soon lay in a wreckage, and at last population estimates began to bear some relation to reality.

Outside the IWC, because of the American administration's refusal to use Pelly Amendment sactions against Japan, the US Senate, to force their hand, passed the Packwood-Magnusson Amendment to the International Fishery Conservation and Management Act. This amendment ruled that any nation violating IWC rulings would be banned from fishing within the US 200-mile limit.

For many of the whaling nations this was a severe sanction. In Japan's case it was unthinkable. Its $40-million whaling industry would cost its fishing industry $500 million in lost fishing rights.

This amendment became the Save the Whale movement's most powerful weapon. As Senator Bob Packwood himself pointed out, the sanctions applied to 'any nation which violates IWC regulations, regardless of that nation's membership within the IWC'. Furthermore those sanctions were not dependent on the whim of administration, but were 'required by US law'. It was a clear directive from the American people to get tough with the whaling nations.

Because of these offensives within and without the IWC, at the 1979 conference there were newly motivated and determined conservationist forces at work. Three major victories were achieved that year at the IWC.

First, conservationists won the greatest quota reductions in IWC history. The quotas fell from 23,520 to 15,656. (In terms of tonnage, it was even more remarkable – nearly 50 per cent – as the majority of the quota was made up of small minke whales.)

Second, a ruling was passed that the entire Indian Ocean be declared a whale sanctuary.

Third, with the exclusion of the small minke whale, there was to be a ban on pelagic whaling. This essentially outlawed all factory ship whaling except for the Soviet and Japanese Antarctic minke whale fishery.

Both on the front line of the Whale War and on the diplomatic front at the IWC, 1979 was the critical turning point in the conflict.

2 FIFTH COLUMNISTS

At the 1981 IWC conference St Lucia made its extraordinary maiden speech in front of the glowering Japanese delegation. The Honourable Peter Josie made an appeal to the commission:

> Generally speaking, the world's whale stocks have decreased since this commission came into existence thirty-three years ago. Until this year, this commission has represented only a small segment of the human family. With the entry of India, China, Dominica, Jamaica, Uruguay and my own country, and the arrival of observers from Kenya, Egypt, Costa Rica and Colombia, this commission has in my view taken a giant step forward in terms of becoming what it should be.
>
> Perhaps the time is now right for us to propose an amendment to the appropriate article to this convention which would specifically declare the whale as our common inheritance. Perhaps the time is also opportune for St Lucia to propose that the IWC become an affiliate of the United Nations under its charter.

Perhaps, but the whalers were near to rioting over the idea and would not allow the proposal a hearing. The Japanese reply was immediate. They would have nothing to do with the United Nations. Furthermore, they would not submit themselves to a 'tyranny of votes' from this sudden avalanche of new members. The whalers could 'never succumb to the violence of such a majority'.

A decade before, at the beginning of the Whale War, the IWC was a 14-member whalers' club, closed to the press and observers, with no permanent staff, meeting annually for two days. Its secretariat was housed in a single filing cabinet in the offices of the UK's Ministry of Agriculture, Fisheries and Food offices. By 1982 it would mushroom to a convention of 37 nations with several hundred delegates, observers and press people – not to mention 20,000 demonstrators. Its secretariat had its own offices in Cambridge and was run by a full-time staff of five. An annual meeting extended to a full week.

Obviously there was a dramatic escalation of the conflict. There was a worldwide call to arms, and in an effort equivalent to moving the mountain to Mohammed, the conservationists decided that if the IWC would not go to the UN, then they would do what they could to move a good part of the UN to the IWC.

How had this happened?

In 1979, a new highly unlikely nation was found to be spearheading the conservationist forces at the IWC. This was the tiny Seychelles, a nation boasting a population of 64,000. It was led by an even more unlikely commissioner, the parapsychologists' guru and author Lyall Watson.

From 1979 to 1982 Watson was the charismatic central figure of the conservationists' new initiatives within the IWC. And it was he, as a Seychelles delegate, who engineered the Indian Ocean Whale Sanctuary scheme. Watson and the Seychelles acted as the public focus for a worldwide recruitment drive for conservationist nations to join the IWC. The Seychelles' Washington DC office was the tactical and funding centre for the drive, and its efficient co-ordinator was the tough and attractive professional activist Cornelia Durrant.

There were as well less public figures working with Watson. The key strategists of the scheme in fact were Watson, Greenpeace International director David McTaggert, and Jean-Paul Fortom-Gouin – who was the chief architect of the pelagic and (later) the sperm whale hunting ban. Other prime movers in this diplomatic initiative were Sir Peter Scott of the World Wildlife Fund, IWC scientist Dr Sidney Holt, Dr Francisco Palacio of Miami's Tinker Institute, Christine Stevens of Washington's Animal Welfare Institute, and several other influential, but intentionally invisible individuals, including Sadrudin Aga Khan.

The call to arms was a remarkable success and, combined with the infiltration of the Scientific Committee and the big stick of the Packwood-Magnusson Amendment, set the stage for the Whale War's D-Day at the 1982 IWC.

Year	Quota	Membership
1972–73	42,500	**14 nations:** United States, Britain, Mexico, France, Argentina, Australia, Canada, Panama, Denmark, Japan, USSR, Norway, Iceland, South Africa
1973–74	40,979	
1974–75	39,864	**15 nations:** Brazil joins
1975–76	32,578	
1976–77	28,050	**16 nations:** New Zealand joins
1977–78	23,520	**17 nations:** Netherlands joins
1978–79	20,428	
1979–80	15,653	**23 nations:** Seychelles, Sweden, Chile, Peru, Spain, Korea join
1980–81	14,523	**24 nations:** Switzerland, Oman join (Panama withdraws)
1981–82	14,233	**32 nations:** Jamaica, St Lucia, Dominica, Costa Rica, Uruguay, China, St Vincent, India, Philippines join (Canada withdraws)
1982–83	12,263	**37 nations:** Egypt, Kenya, Senegal, Belize, Antigua, Monaco, Germany join (Jamaica, Dominica withdraw)
1983–84	9,390	**39 nations:** Finland, Mauritius join
1984–85	6,623	
1985–86	0	**41 nations:** Ireland, Solomon Islands join

Figure 8.1 The International Whaling Commission 1972–86: Membership recruitment

3 MORATORIUM VICTORY

In the early 1960s, long before the Whale War came to popular attention, a giant white rubber sperm whale stopped all traffic as it was led through the streets of Brighton down to the sea. This was no protest march; it was a full-size model of a white whale created in an English film studio in preparation for *Moby Dick* – 'soon to be a major motion picture'. The Brighton piers were to be the setting for that epic struggle between Ahab and the whale.

But the best-laid schemes of film directors and special effects experts often go astray. One dark and stormy night, the sea grew so rough that Moby Dick was torn from its moorings and swept out into the English Channel. There, the bobbing white phantom loose in its element created chaos in the world's busiest shipping lane. For a short time the reincarnated Moby Dick was nearly as much of a hazard to navigation as its legendary prototype.

For reasons unrelated to *Moby Dick: the Film*, the 1982 IWC meeting was held in Brighton for the third year running, in the Metropole Hotel on the picturesque Regency waterfront. Between the two Brighton piers, with their delicate wedding-cake architecture elegantly crumbling into the sea, protesters made their siege encampment. Out on the water two Greenpeace ships, the *Cedarlea* and the *Syrius*, stood like gunboats in silent vigil, awaiting the critical vote.

Ten years of campaigning within and without the IWC had brought them to await the decisive outcome of the Seychelles' motion for the moratorium vote – a ten-year cessation of all commercial whaling, with a three-year phasing-out period, ending by the 1985–86 whaling season.

Despite last-minute attempts to sabotage the Scientific Committee, and tantrums and threats from the Japanese, the votes came in like a rolling artillery barrage. The whalers' defence did not hold. Only the USSR, Japan, Norway, Peru, Iceland, Brazil and Korea voted no. The final vote was 25 to 7 – with 5 abstaining. The needed three-quarters majority had been achieved.

Inside the Metropole crowds of delegates and observers, and outside crowds of demonstrators, jumped up and down, shouting and cheering. More than a few champagne corks popped. On the pavement a crowd of demonstrators cheered and waved as a van with a blue papier-mâché whale on its roof drove by, its loudspeakers blaring out whale song. It had a 'Save the Whales' sign on it. Below this was a new banner, 'Whales Saved – Brighton 1982'.

It should have been the end of the Whale War. Unfortunately, it was not. To understand why, it is perhaps necessary to understand something of the major advocate of whaling: Japan.

Conservationists	Whalers
1979	1979–80 quota: 15,653
• Factory ship ban – IWC bans pelagic whaling except for minke whales • Indian Ocean whale sanctuary – IWC ban on all whaling in Indian Ocean • Science initiative at IWC Science Committee • Packwood–Magnusson Amendment in US threatens all IWC violators with banning of fishing rights within US 200-mile limit [*Sea Shepherd* rams pirate ship *Sierra*] [*Rainbow Warrior* in Icelandic and Spanish actions] [*Sea Shepherd* scuttled in Portugal]	• IWC – 23 nations: former pirate whalers Chile, Peru, Spain and Korea join. Also conservationists Seychelles and Sweden • Japan bans import of non-IWC meat under US pressure – immediate violations • Spanish, Peruvian, Chilean, Japanese, Russian, Korean, Icelandic, Norwegian violations • Brazil passes Edict N–017 to end whaling, but Japanese economic pressure prevents its use • Taiwanese pirates exposed – thousands of tons of pirate meat smuggled into Japan • Russian sperm whale and orca violations
1980	1980–81 quota: 14,523
• IWC – 24 nations: Switzerland, Oman join • World conservation strategy – UNEP, IUCN, WWF recommend whaling moratorium • Ethics of Whaling Conference [*Rainbow Warrior* captured by Spanish navy, but later escapes custody]	• Sperm whale ban fails at IWC because Canada betrays conservationists and votes with whalers • Panama forced out of IWC by Japanese pressure [Pirate blitz: *Sierra* sunk in Portugal; *Ibsa I* and *II* sunk in Spain; *Susan* and *Theresa* seized in South Africa; *Sea Bird, Sea Flower, Chu Feng, Chi Hsin* seized in Taiwan]
1981	1981–82 quota: 14,233
• IWC – 32 nations: Jamaica, St Lucia, Dominica, Costa Rica, Uruguay, China, India, St Vincent, Philippines join (Canada withdraws) • Sperm whale ban – vote 25–1. (2-year phase out period to 1984) [*Sea Shepherd II* invades Siberia]	• Japanese floating factory violation debated • Korean whale meat 'laundry' closed • Chilean illegal factory ship violation debated
1982	1982–83 quota: 12,263
• IWC – 37 nations: Egypt, Kenya, Senegal, Belize, Antigua, Monaco, Germany join • IWC moratorium victory – vote 25–7–5. 10-year ban on commercial whaling with 3-year phase-out period to 1985–86 • EEC ban on all whale products after extended FOE campaign [*Rainbow Warrior* Peru action]	• Philippines switch to whaling nation. Operate illegal factory ship • Jamaica, Dominica forced out of IWC by Japanese economic pressure

Conservationists	Whalers
1983	1983–84 quota: 9,390
• IWC – 39 nations: Finland, Mauritius join [*Rainbow Warrior* in Siberian actions]	• Further violations by Philippines, Chile, Japan, etc.
1984	1984–85 quota: 6,623
• Court victory (November) – conservationists sue US government for not invoking Packwood–Magnusson sanctions on Japan. Win, but government wins delay by appealing case	• Japanese–American deal. Japan violates sperm whale ban, but makes bilateral deal with US to avoid sanctions. Also 2nd deal to allow whaling until 1988 • Russia exceeds IWC quotas by 1,000 whales. Suffers sanctions under Packwood–Magnusson Amendment • Peru and Iceland withdraw objections to moratorium
1985	1985–86 quota: 0
• IWC – 41 nations: Ireland, Solomon Islands join • Moratorium on commercial whaling comes into effect. Zero quotas, but 3 nations defy it, and 2 nations use loophole to avoid it • 2nd court victory (August) – conservationists again win case against government refusal to invoke Packwood–Magnusson sanctions on Japan, but again government wins delay by appealing [sinking of *Rainbow Warrior* by French agents in New Zealand] [Faroes Islands action by EIA against pilot whale slaughter]	• Japan, Russia, Norway object to moratorium and continue whaling beyond 1986 • Iceland, Korea – loophole whaling – use ruse of 'scientific permits' to continue hunt past 1986. Unilateral quotas set, but whales still sold to Japan • USSR promises end to whaling 1987 • Ireland and Solomon Islands join IWC days before IWC in order to lend support to US administration plans for bowhead Eskimo quotas and deals with Japan
1986	1986–87 quota: 0
• 3rd court hearing – defeat (July) Final Supreme Court decision on Packwood–Magnusson sanctions. Under pressure from Reagan administration the court defeats the amendment by the narrowest 5–4 ruling [*Sea Shepherd* saboteurs sink the two Icelandic whalers *Hvalur VI* and *Hvalur VII*, and demolish the Hvalfjordur whale processing plant]	• Japan, Russia set own quotas independent of IWC and continue whaling • Norway – loophole whaling – joins 'scientific whaling' bandwagon • St Lucia, St Vincent and Trinidad sack their pro-conservationist delegates

Figure 8.2 The International Whaling Commission 1979–86

9

INTRIGUES OF THE SAMURAI

1 THE NEMAWASHI

'Strategy is the craft of the warrior,' wrote the sixteenth-century samurai Miyamoto Musashi. Musashi the Kensai, or 'sword saint', was Japan's most renowned warrior who late in his life wrote the *Go Rin No Sho*, the *Book of Five Rings*. For three centuries, Musashi's book has been the bible of Japanese interested in the art and science of strategy. In war, in politics and even in business practices, the Japanese have been informed by the strategies of Musashi. The way of the samurai can certainly be observed in the manœuvrings of the Japanese delegation to the International Whaling Commission. There is little doubt by any concerned with the IWC that the Japanese are the master strategists of the pro-whaling forces.

As Musashi wrote: 'It is said the warrior's is twofold Way of pen and sword, and he should have a taste for both Ways.' This was certainly the strategy of the whalers. If the direct approach of the sword (or perhaps more appropriately, the harpoon) was blocked, the creative wielding of the pen would be used as a weapon to gain the advantage. So armed, the strategists among the whalers have won many battles.

It is startlingly instructive to look at a little of the recent history of the Japanese exertion of diplomatic and economic pressure in the Whale War to realize just how strong is their commitment in this struggle.

After the conservationist blitzkrieg on the pirates and the infiltration of the IWC Scientific Committee in 1979 and 1980, there was a massive retreat of the whaling forces on all fronts. However, the Japanese in particular rose to the challenge. Recognizing that the new strategic centre of the environmental forces' power block was, extraordinarily enough, the tiny nation of the Seychelles, they soon directed an attack on that country.

Prime Minister Zenko Suzuki focused all his attention on the whaling issue. Suzuki is a tough old campaigner whose primary purpose in thirty years of politics has been to give the fishing industry everything it wants. The fishing and whaling industry are his personal power base, and he has no intention of giving way. His style of fighting is not confrontational. Indeed, his own rise to power was through his skill as a backroom politician. He is known in Japan as a master *nemawashi* – 'one who is skilled in manœuvring behind the scenes' – or as westerners would term him, a 'fixer'. And it was his skills as a nemawashi that he brought to bear on the problematic Seychelles conspiracy.

Suzuki and his government had dealt many times with such small Third World countries as the Seychelles, and it was usually only a matter of subtly placing the right amount of pressure (usually economic) in the right place. The Seychelles, a nation with severe financial problems, seemed particularly vulnerable. Consequently, a suitable economic sanction was found conveniently at hand early in 1980. In the offing was a Japanese grant scheme which would allow the Seychelles to acquire a fisheries research-training vessel. The Japanese ambassador left no room for doubt about the reason for possible withdrawal of the grant scheme. It was an approach which, along with several other acts of 'persuasion' of Third World countries over the whaling issue, prompted the *South China Morning Post* to run a full-page article headed 'BLACKMAIL! Japan's Last Desperate Tactic'.

The letter from the Japanese ambassador read:

My government is facing difficulties in co-ordinating divergent views concerning the extension of such a grant to your country. In particular, the fishery industry in Japan strongly oppose the grant in view of your government's attitude at the IWC.

Therefore, in view of this, all I can say at this time is that if in future your government should change its attitude at the IWC towards Japan, there would be a possibility of my government extending the grant to Seychelles.

In this move, however, the Japanese had very much under-estimated the resolve of the Seychelles on this issue. Its government had made conservation a part of its national platform and international image, so much so that at the 1980 Moscow Olympics, when the Seychelles – as the smallest and therefore first delegation – marched into the stadium, the television announcers called it the 'environmentalist nation of the Seychelles'.

The Japanese were soon to find that, albeit small and poor, they were dealing with a very proud country with not a little courage. The Seychelles Minister of Development and Planning, Maxine Ferrari, replied quickly with considerable indignation at this system of foreign aid: 'Such a situation does not represent co-operation but domination.'

At length another minister wrote:

In this particular case, the Ministry of Foreign Affairs regrets to note that the Japanese government, whilst expressing annoyance with Seychelles' positive stand in IWC, did not take into consideration the indiscriminate and rapacious exploitation of the Seychelles fisheries resources by the Japanese fishing fleet over many years in the recent past. Making Japanese advanced technology available to Seychelles to sort out the mess left behind by Japanese fishermen would constitute but a meagre form of restitution.

Far from being intimidated, the Seychelles government will continue to speak in the interest of Seychelles and other Third World countries on its position *vis-à-vis* Japan.

These statements were followed by an action that would ensure there was no doubt about the Seychelles's seriousness on the matter. On 9 January 1981 the Japanese 299-ton fishing boat *Number 25 Sumi Maru* was seized while fishing within the Seychelles waters. The fines mounted against it – US $115,000 – sent a very clear message to Tokyo.

Realizing they had made an error in judgment of their tiny opponent, Prime Minister Suzuki and his colleagues rethought their strategy. They came to a consensus and on April Fool's day

1982 arranged a meeting between the Seychelles Minister of Development and Planning, Maxine Ferrari, and Prime Minister Suzuki to talk about foreign aid *and* whaling. Ferrari then experienced a first-hand encounter with the most accomplished *nemawashi* in Asia; it was a breathtaking meeting for the Seychelles minister.

It appeared that Mr Suzuki understood that for the Seychelles the whaling issue was a matter of principle and honour, and the Japanese move at sanctions had been a rather cheap attempt to compromise their position. This of course would never do; the Seychelles had proved itself a brave opponent, and a brave opponent did not sell its honour cheaply. The fisheries grant scheme had been an insulting offer. Honour did not come cheap: so how about an aid package of about $40 million?

Despite his own resolve on the whaling issue, the Seychelles minister came out of the meeting staggering. He knew that with his country in its current financial straits, this was an offer he couldn't refuse, or at least an offer he couldn't refuse on his own authority. And so he packed up from the meeting and took the aid package back to his own cabinet for discussion.

As one Seychelles delegate to the IWC was later to remark, it had been 'a very, very close thing'. The Japanese believed the Seychelles would soon be in their pocket at the IWC, and in fact one Tokyo newspaper, *Asashi Shimbun*, even reported that the Seychelles had definitely decided to change its IWC position and withdraw its proposed tabling of the whaling moratorium.

But once again Suzuki's *nemawashi* tactics did not work. Amazingly, the Seychelles government ministers stood their ground against the Japanese offer. No, they said, the deal was off. The moratorium would be tabled.

2 THE KUROMAKU

Although certainly not unknown in the west, Japanese politicians have what seems an inordinate fondness for the tradition of the puppet Shogun controlled at half a dozen removes by some minor minister. If the term *nemawashi* or fixer is necessary to understand one aspect of Japanese tactics, an even more important term is *kuromaku* which translates as 'string-puller behind the scene'. The *kuromaku* is the puppet-master and king-maker, the mastermind behind the ruler. In Japan, for the last two decades (until his recent illness) the master *kuromaku* has been Kakuei Tanaka who, because of his criminal indictment in 1974, has had to take a backstage position. It was for Tanaka, the godfather of Japanese politics, that Suzuki served as an able second-in-command fixer for many years.

By nature a fixer has no real policies or ideas of his own, which of course is exactly why Tanaka eventually made Suzuki Prime Minister. Through Suzuki, Tanaka's interests would not be neglected; and neither would the interests of the lesser *kuromaku*, the tycoons of the fishing and whaling industry, each of whom had their own string attached to their puppet Prime Minister.

In Japan, with the *kuromaku* and the *nemawashi* diligently at work, we seem to have political intrigue essentially viewed as an art form. And as such, in the sphere of whaling issues in the Third World, it seems to be Japan's primary cultural export item. The Seychelles was not the only Third World beneficiary of *kuromaku* and *nemawashi* tactics that one environmentalist summed up as: 'If you can't beat them, then buy them.'

A classic example presented itself in 1978, when Panama was the only IWC member to ask for a moratorium vote at the meeting. Suddenly, just one day before the meeting opened, Panama's IWC commissioner, Jean Paul Fortom-Gouin received a direct order from his minister to immediately withdraw both himself and the moratorium from the agenda. Restored to the Panama delegation in 1979, Fortom-Gouin managed to instigate the pelagic whaling ban. However, this act resulted in Panama not only unseating Fortom-Gouin again but withdrawing its delegation entirely from the convention. The deputy commissioner to Panama later stated privately the reason for the sudden switch: Japan had threatened to cancel a $5 million sugar order unless Panama withdrew the moratorium motion. Unlike the Seychelles a few years later, Panama immediately complied.

Brazil provided a similar but more lucrative example. In 1979 it decided to close down its whaling operations as outlined in Edict N-017. In no uncertain terms it was to take an anti-whaling stance for both conservationist and ethical reasons. Brazilian ecologists hailed this as a victory for their cause, and a death-blow to the Japanese-controlled Brazilian whaling industry. However, because of Japanese trade pressure that explicit ban was reversed by order of the President in 1980.

In 1981 Brazil abstained from the moratorium vote, and again informed the IWC that it was getting out of the whaling business that year. In 1982 it not only remained in the business as a Japanese whaling colony but changed its abstention to a no vote against the moratorium, thus totally betraying those who drafted Edict N-017.

The Brazilian newspaper *Folha de Sao Paulo* made it absolutely clear why the decision had been made. Japan had offered Brazil a $400-million agricultural investment programme, which involved an expectation that Brazil would reach a sympathetic 'understanding' of Japan's position on whaling. Brazil was abundantly 'understanding'. Conservationists in Peru and Chile have similar tales of Japanese 'foreign aid' and trade negotiations. South Korea's attitude towards understanding the Japanese was not a little affected by a $4 billion credit extension. And most environmentalists are convinced that the disappearance in 1982 of Jamaica and its commissioner Allan Isaacs, after his strong conservationist stance the year before, was directly linked to Japanese negotiations to purchase 95 per cent of Jamaica's Blue Mountain coffee crop.

Jamaica never again rejoined the IWC, while new IWC nations like Dominica and Uruguay made only one appearance each as conservationist delegates before Japanese pressure intimidated them into vanishing. Costa Rica and the Philippines, offered proper incentives, simply switched entirely from conservationist to pro-whaling stances. The big persuasive offers were also matched with little perks for individuals. As one senior commissioner at the IWC said: 'If you are a conservationist commissioner and want to visit Japan with your family, all you have to do is say "yes" – especially if you are willing to go during a commission meeting.'

Such offers were made to Seychelles delegates, and Jamaican commissioner Allan Isaacs was invited to go to Japan on an expenses-paid trip that would coincidentally not have allowed him to attend a special commission meeting in March 1981 to consider the Japanese sperm whale kill. Isaacs graciously declined the offer.

Some manœuvres remain something of a mystery. What incentive, for instance, was there for the extraordinary betrayal of the conservationists by Canadian in the 1980 sperm whale hunt ban? Canada astonished everyone by switching sides and voting with the whalers. The ban failed by that one critical vote. However, this switch caused so much outrage domestically that Canada withdrew as a voting member of the commission in 1981.

When Geoffrey Lean, the London *Observer*'s environmental correspondent questioned Japan's commissioner Kunio Yonezawa, and cited many of the arm-twisting tactics used by Japan, Yonezawa, incensed, denied all allegations. 'My conscience is very clear. My country is not that sort of country. It is very decent. We have done certain things to persuade these governments, but only by talks.'

3 THE KILL THE WHALE LOBBY

The tactics of the *nemawashi* and the *kuromaku*, however, were not limited to the Third World. Recognizing that America still was Japan's most dangerous foe in the Whale War because of the possibility of fishing and trade sanctions, the string-pullers and fixers were hard at work in Washington.

Motonobu Inagaki, president of the Japanese Nippon Hogei Whaling Company, quite plainly stated in a *Japan Times* interview in October 1981 that if Japan could not achieve what it wished at the IWC, the way was clear: 'we have to hold backstage negotiations in more earnest among the whaling nations and some of the main anti-whaling countries, particularly the US, to reach a compromise.' What did Inagaki consider a reasonable 'compromise'? Simply an agreed strategy by which 'the US may shut one eye, if not both eyes, to Japan's whaling'.

Among the more startling Japanese moves during this period was the hiring of the extremely compromising former US IWC commissioner 'Big Dick' Frank by his supposed adversary, Japanese commissioner Yonezawa. Frank registered as a 'foreign agent' and in June 1982 received an initial payment of $30,000, soon followed by a further $43,000, as an adviser to the Japanese.

Frank had formally joined the ranks of that growing army of mercenaries within America who worked for Japanese pay, which *Mother Jones* magazine labelled the 'Kill the Whale Lobby'. The most highly visible registered 'foreign agent' of this gang of mercenaries was and is Alan Macnow, a New York-based public relations man and lobbyist. For the twelve months from

March 1981 to March 1982, Macnow's fees paid by the Japanese Whaling Association and the Japanese Fishing Association were a modest $347,000, thank you very much, and have risen steadily each year since then. But of course Macnow was not alone. That same year a former aide to Alaskan Senator Ted Stevens received at least $172,000 from the JWA and the JFA for his advisory services.

The extent of Japan's lobbying power in Washington is quite startling. And so far as the whaling issue is concerned, it seems quite insidious because of the extremely close government-industry connections, which in many cases would be considered illegal in America because of obvious conflict of interests which would be construed as government corruption. It is further complicated by the monolithic nature of government and industry in Japan.

An example is the fact that Japan's IWC commissioner Kunio Yonezawa was also a paid consultant of the Nippon Suisan Whaling Company until he resigned in 1984 and was then employed full-time by Nippon Suisan. It has been something of a tradition, in fact, for the Japan IWC commissioner to also be the president of the Japanese Whaling Association. (The Animal Welfare Institute has pointed out that this is roughly equivalent to the American negotiator in the car trade treaty agreements being a paid consultant of General Motors.)

The Japanese whaling industry is largely controlled by the giant Taiyo Fishing Company, which in turn is controlled by the biggest company in all Asia, Mitsubishi, whose tentacles reach everywhere in America. And when it comes to lobbying ability, the Japanese have proved second to none.

Representative James R. Jones, one of the Japan experts on the US House Ways and Means Subcommittee on Trade, commented in 1980: 'We used to say that the British and then the Israelis were the best-briefed politicians. Now it's the Japanese.'

Japan follows the standard employment practice that in Washington is known as the 'revolving door' – that is, they employ former government figures who have moved out of office into the private sector. As government figures – and while employed by the government – it would have been unethical for them to receive money from lobbyists. However, once out of office – and while retaining connections in Congress, the Executive Branch or within various government departments –

it seems perfectly all right to be employed as an adviser.

In 1981 former Transport Secretary Brock Adams, whose former job included directing the Coast Guard to enforce the US 200-mile fishing limit, was being employed at $60,000 a year to protect Japanese fishing and whaling interests *within* that zone.

The monies paid out were considerable. In 1980 Robert Keefe, an adviser and fund raiser for the Democratic Party, received the sum of $80,000 from the Japan Whaling Association. Since 1984 the Japanese whaling interests have found ready advocates in such US Congressmen as Mervyn Dymally. Shortly before the 1985 IWC meeting at which he was frankly labelled 'the Japanese mouthpiece' on the US delegation, Dymally had flown out to the Japanese whaling town of Taiji, where he gave a remarkable speech which abused the IWC for its 'unreasonable' position. 'The anti-whaling movement,' Dymally stated, 'is run by some environmentalists who do not reflect the voice of the US public.' Furthermore, he said, 'There are Congressmen who are interested in the whaling issue in the US Congress. A continuation of whaling will be a long fight, but you must not give up. . . . I will appeal for you in the US Congress for the continuation of whaling.'

Advisers for other Japanese interests have included at one time or another Richard Allen, Reagan foreign policy adviser; William D. Eberle, President Ford's chief trade negotiator; Frank A. Weil, former Assistant Commerce Secretary for International Trade; Daniel Minchew, former chairman of the International Trade Commission; and Robert Angel, director of the US–Japan Trade Council.

Well over 100 foreign agents for Japan are registered in Washington by the Justice Department – far more than for any other nation – with a similar number of Japanese media representatives.

In the face of its lobbying muscle, one particular Japanese piece of propaganda directed against the ecologists has always struck them as very odd indeed. This is the accusation that Greenpeace in particular is a CIA front that is using the whole issue for an attack on Japan that is basically racist and economic in motivation. The reason ecologists find this particular smear strange is that by 1980 the front running Kill the Whale adviser to the Japanese whaling interests proved to be none other than former CIA director William Colby. As spokesman for the

Japanese organization called the Centre for Political Public Relations, for $150 an hour Colby reported to the Japanese on the anti-whaling campaign in the US. No doubt ex-director Colby has access to the best possible intelligence on the movement, and the Japanese are willing to pay for the very best.

10

HOME FRONT: JAPAN

1 DEFENCE SYSTEMS

'Know your enemy' is a basic in any military campaign. However, in the Japanese whaling industry, this is more easily said than done. The tenacity of the industry in the face of universal condemnation, its cost to Japan's image abroad and its costs in threatened economic sanctions and boycotts is remarkable. It all seems somewhat puzzling and frankly 'inscrutable' to many environmentalists, some of whom are Japanese themselves.

If we take a look at the six-point public defence of the whaling industry, there does seem to be a certain logic involved.

(1) Japan's whaling industry, like any other legitimate industry, creates wealth for the benefit of the nation.
(2) The whaling industry provides an income for 50,000 Japanese.
(3) Whale meat is a traditional part of the Japanese diet.
(4) Whale meat is essential protein for a protein-poor nation.
(5) The Japanese people are entirely supportive of the whaling industry.
(6) The anti-whaling movement is a thinly veiled racist, anti-Japanese movement.

A closer look at these statements reveals some patent untruths.

(1) *Japan's whaling industry, like any other legitimate industry,*

creates wealth for the benefit of the nation. In fact, the industry is bankrupt. In 1979, when times were better, Motonobu Inagaki, president of Japan's Joint Whaling Company, admitted it had accumulated deficits of 300 million yen despite massive government grants and loans. The industry loses money continuously despite the government's direct and indirect subsidies, which are estimated to be in excess of US $10 million each year.

(2) *The whaling industry provides an income for 50,000 Japanese.* In fact, the figure for full-time employment in the industry is certainly less than 2,500, while some environmental groups quote figures under 1,000. The figure of 50,000 widely quoted in the Japanese press was creatively compiled by an industry spokesman; it included whalers, their extended families and every clerk or market trader (and their extended families) who incidentally handled a can or piece of whale meat in the course of their jobs.

(3) *Whale meat is a traditional part of the Japanese diet.* In fact for most Japanese it is a tradition which extends back as far as 1950. Apart from a handful of coastal fishing villages where subsistence whaling was traditionally conducted, widespread consumption of whale meat hardly existed in Japan until after the Second World War.

(4) *Whale meat is essential protein for a protein-poor nation.* In fact, whale meat provides less than 1 per cent of the protein in the Japanese diet, and by some estimates less than one-tenth of 1 per cent. Japan is not protein-poor. Japan is a net exporter of its primary protein source, fish. Japanese tuna exports alone are equal to many times the whale meat consumed by the nation.

(5) *The Japanese people are entirely supportive of the whaling industry.* In fact, the majority of the Japanese people are fairly neutral on the issue. Remarkably, however, when in 1983 one Gallup/Nippon poll ran a survey on whaling with the question 'Should Japan object to the IWC's moratorium and continue whaling, or should it accept the decision?', 76 per cent of the Japanese population thought it should 'accept the decision'. Only 17 per cent thought Japan should continue whaling.

(6) *The anti-whaling movement is a thinly veiled racist, anti-Japanese movement.* This unfounded accusation has absurdly won more converts than any of the other defences. Offering absolutely no evidence of this perceived racism, the Japanese Whaling Association publishes stacks of glossy brochures for

journalists and others which read: 'Anti-Japan sentiment is at the root of the world's anti-whaling mood.' The whaling issue is said to be only an excuse for Europeans and Americans who are prejudiced against 'races other than their own, especially the yellow race'. Or as Takashi Atoda, author, Japanese Whaling Commission and IWC delegate, stated in the Japanese press: 'Because white people have contempt for the yellow race, they want an excuse to say that Japan, whose economy has expanded in recent times, is barbarian.'

It is an argument that in itself intentionally arouses racist sentiments and urges the Japanese public to rally around the oppressed 'yellow man'. Besides sidestepping the whole issue of whaling itself, it also ignores the fact that if the movement is anti-Japanese, it must also be anti-Norwegian, anti-Icelandic and anti-Soviet – all nations not generally thought of as being run by the 'yellow race'.

2 SPOILS OF WAR

The economics of the whaling industry for the past three decades at least has been entirely governed by the Japanese market for whale meat. Until that market was opened after the Second World War, whaling was carried out almost entirely for the extraction of whale oil for such products as margarine and soap. The meat was discarded.

Japan makes much play of its ancient tradition of whaling, however, historic records reveal that from the seventeenth until the twentieth century the average annual catch was less than 20 whales. It was not until 1934, in fact, that the small-scale coastal village industry expanded and Japan acquired a modern pelagic whaling fleet. By 1939 it had six factory vessels with which it plundered the southern oceans. During this time and until 1941 and the war that destroyed the fleet, the Japanese refused to sign or abide by any international agreements to control its killing.

The reason for this intractability was not the need for food. At that time Japan discarded the meat as other nations did, and simply extracted the oil, firstly because there was no real market for the meat in Japan, and secondly because the fleet was owned by the Nippon Suisan Kabushiki Kaisha Company, whose main shareholder was the Manchurian Heavy Industry Corporation, the principal economic and industrial arm of the Japanese army in Manchuria. The sole purpose of the Japanese whaling industry at that time was to supply foreign currency for the army at war in Manchuria. Oil was therefore extracted from the whales, and since by law it was forbidden to be imported into Japan, it was sold to Europe, and the foreign currency was fuel for the Manchurian war.

In the 1950s, after the war, whaling began in earnest. There was a genuine protein shortage in the immediate post-war years; any kind of protein was welcome, and for the first time in its history urban Japan developed a market for whale meat, although at no time did whale meat exceed 2 per cent of the animal protein in the Japanese diet. It was only after that most critical period had passed, when in fact the fishing industry began to export its particular protein source, that the Japanese whaling industry began its rapid expansion. Fed by huge government loans, grants and subsidies, the industry kept growing from 1956 to 1966, despite the consequent collapse of whale populations. The tactics during this period were extraordinarily cut-throat, and Japanese pressure combined with falling whale stocks drove every pelagic fleet – except the Soviets' – to the wall.

By 1972, then, only the Japanese and the Soviet pelagic fleets hunted in the Antarctic. However, the destruction of whale stocks caused the Japanese to cut back and conglomerate. In 1976, six whaling companies formed Nippon Kyodo Hogei Kaisha Ltd, also known as the Japan Joint Whaling Company. Its three largest shareholders, Taiyo, Nippon Suisan and Kyokuyo, came together to form a single Antarctic pelagic fleet, while its three lesser shareholders, Nippon Hogei, Nitto Hogei and Hokuyo Hogei, hunted with coastal ships in the North Pacific.

By far the largest of the whaling companies is Taiyo, which is owned by the Taiyo Fishing Company. Taiyo Fishing, which is controlled by the Nakabe family, is the largest fishing company in the world and the 67th largest industrial corporation outside the US, enjoying annual sales over US $6 billion. It owns or controls at least 500 ships and has subsidiaries and partnerships in over 20 nations. Furthermore, it is tied into the Mitsubishi Corporation, the largest corporation in all Asia by many times.

It is these whaling companies, and particularly the Taiyo Fishing Company and the multi-millionaire Nakabe family that.

the Japanese government has felt it must protect from the 'crushing' blow of ending the whaling industry.

It was quite apparent that under its own steam the whaling industry would have died out in the late 1960s. To prevent this, the Japanese government began subsidizing the high fuel costs of the Antarctic fleet. Then, too, it subsidized the industry through government-supported price regulations. The government bought the majority of the meat at artificially high prices for government food programmes. The meat was fed to groups who had no choice in their food: convicts, soldiers and schoolchildren.

The absurdity of this is that it is clearly far more economical and practical for the government to buy Australian beef or New Zealand lamb than whale meat which is generally of lower quality and far more expensive.

Although most urban Japanese disdain whale meat, others do consider it a delicacy. Unfortunately, the high-quality end of the whale meat market is very profitable. A choice whale steak will sell in supermarkets for US $25 or more, and raw quality tail meat called 'ono-mi' in suishi restaurants is very expensive indeed.

However, it is the artificially inflated government-determined prices that keep the industry going, that enable the whaling companies to make a profit by marketing not only their own meat but also that of the Russians and all other whaling nations. It is a profit won by the powerful corporations getting politicians to subsidize them out of Japanese taxes.

3 THE POLITICS OF EXTINCTION

The Japanese are not entirely wrong in stating that they have been singled out and 'targeted' by the environmentalists in the Save the Whale movement. For even though the Russians and the pirates have come in for more direct action in confrontation at sea, everyone in the movement has no option but to recognize that Japan is the key nation in the conflict. This has nothing to do with racism.

In hard practical terms, without the Japanese whale meat market, whaling would cease worldwide overnight. But just how to achieve this has presented the environmentalists with major obstacles. Many of them now claim that they have indeed made tactical errors in their approach to Japan because they failed to recognize the massively monolithic nature of Japanese industry and politics, and they failed to anticipate that the Japanese would read the vilification of an industry that is exterminating whales as a vilification of the Japanese government and, by extension, of the Japanese people.

However, the real reasons for the tenacious nature of the government support of the industry has nothing to do with international image, or any of the stated arguments. It is really to do with domestic politics. It is due to the nature of representative democracy in general, and the Japanese system in particular. It is a situation environmentalists have to face again and again when dealing with environmental issues and governments.

Simply stated, even if the majority of the Japanese population were in favour of ending whaling, this would have little real weight in a government that is elected district by district. In districts where whaling is not practised, it is an issue of little or no importance on a local platform; while in districts where whaling *is* practised, anyone opposed to whaling will immediately lose that district. Consequently, the national government will be swayed by minority opinion and can safely ignore the majority. Even if it is simply a matter of five whaling districts nationally, the government knows that it will lose those five if it opposes whaling, while it knows equally that there is no chance at all that an anti-whaling view will win a single new seat elsewhere. Similar situations occur in Canada with the harp seal issue in Newfoundland, and to a lesser degree in the United States with the bowhead whale hunt in Alaska.

The system of representative democracy generally preferred by environmentalists is one like the West German system, whereby geographically elected seats are supplemented by seats determined by popular national votes. In consequence, the West German government is the first in the world to have an elected ecology party in any position of power at all. Its Green Party has managed to realize a large enough popular vote to achieve a 'faction' in the government.

The rule of thumb, when dealing with representative democracies, unfortunately is: national popular opinion does not sway government opinion; but intense regional prejudice does. In Japan the whaling issue is further complicated by the fact that the coastal prefectures (which have intense regional prejudices on whaling) have an abnormally large voting power in the Diet – Japan's parliament.

Furthermore, there is the specifically Japanese way of combining government and industry interests in politics that non-Japanese view as highly dubious. If one is looking for an explanation for the extraordinary influence of the whaling industry in Japanese politics, one must look closely at one man: Zenko Suzuki.

4 MR FISH

Since 1955 Japanese politics has been dominated by the Liberal Democrat party, and in all that time the dedicated figure of Zenko Suzuki has been at work, mostly invisibly behind the scenes. For all of this time Suzuki has been a formidable backroom politician whose activities have led to the building and destruction of many a political career, from backbenchers to Prime Ministers. Suzuki's power base is the wealthy and all-important fishing industry, whose favour and large contributions to political campaigns no Japanese government can ignore.

Suzuki was born into a fishing family in Yamada on the Pacific side of Honshu. He was educated at a fisheries college and then employed by a leading fishing industrialist as a private secretary. Later he became the chairman of the fishermen's union and then was elected to the Diet shortly after the war.

In the conservative politics of the Liberal Democrats Suzuki was thought to lack the wealth, connections and university training considered necessary for the more important cabinet posts such as finance or foreign trade and industry. However, none could rival Suzuki's position as the chief spokesman for the fishing industry. Since his appearance in the Liberal Democrat ranks, Suzuki has proudly carried the nickname Mr Fish.

Access to the huge financial resources of the fishing industry, as the *New York Times* once wrote, 'provided him with funds – always needed in ample quantities in often corrupt conservative politics – and gave him great strength as a no. 2 leader.' Indeed, Suzuki's power to make backroom deals, combined with his long-term alliance with the disgraced 'godfather' of Japanese politics, Kakuei Tanaka, resulted in 1980 in the most extraordinary series of manipulations of his career. In the midst of a particularly nasty and chaotic leadership race, virtually everyone involved, except the all-knowing Tanaka, was astonished that the ubiquitous Mr Fish emerged as the new Prime Minister over the heads of all the more obvious front runners.

His colleagues were correct: Suzuki was not a brilliant front man. However, he did take full advantage of his position as Prime Minister to defend all fishing interests, including the whaling industry, as demonstrated in the Seychelles 'persuasion' incident.

By 1982 Suzuki was no longer Prime Minister, but in reality he was no less powerful in his influence. He was diligently back at work behind the scenes.

Protecting the whaling industry has virtually nothing to do with its ability to acquire wealth for the nation. (Indeed, to give some idea of proportion, it might be worth noting that by 1972, the Japanese seaweed industry was worth three times as much as the whaling industry.) For Suzuki it is a means of demonstrating his loyalty, and to this end he is willing to have the government and the taxpayers spend millions to keep it going. Wasteful though this may be, no one within the government dares to effectively oppose the wishes of Mr Fish for fear it will create an immediate cash flow problem for the offender.

The tenor of Suzuki as an opponent was seen when he took on the most feared and thankless job in Japanese politics. With apparent enthusiasm at the idea of defending his pet industry, he gladly entered negotiations with the Russians for fishing rights in the Sea of Okhotsk. At the end of a marathon 45-day negotiation, Suzuki emerged bright as a mackerel with the worn-out Russian delegates to announce a satisfactory quota. Such is the tenacity of the Save the Whale movement's chief opponent. It is a tenacity they must be prepared to match if they wish to win their cause.

5 LOGISTICS

These, then, are the reasons why Suzuki and other politicians fight to save the whaling industry, and the reasons why middlemen and pirate whalers are profiting from an artificially inflated whale meat market. What is perhaps not clear is why those backing the large-scale whaling fleets wish to hang on to the bitter end. If Japanese whaling creates no real wealth, employs few people, contributes little to the food supply, has little place in tradition and has little popular support, what conceivable reason can there be for its continuation?

The answer is that in a cold-blooded mathematical calculation, the yearly loss of the industry is less than the cost of closing down the industry – and the yearly loss may be covered by government subsidy and loans. The single most expensive aspect of the industry close-down would be the implementation of the Japanese severance pay system. This system would require an average payment of more than US $30,000 per laid-off worker. Added to this would be the cost of either scrapping the whaling fleet or refitting it for other purposes.

Frustrated by what is seen as corrupt internal politics keeping a bankrupt industry alive, many conservationists have looked for a similarly cold-blooded mathematical way to inflict financial damage on its backers. Some Save the Whale campaigners, only partially understanding the basic economics of the whaling industry, have advocated total consumer boycotts of Japanese goods. One such man is the biologist and activist Wolf Durr, who is in the habit of turning up during Japanese state visits and committing ritual public executions of Toyotas, plunging harpoons into the cars.

'Save a Whale – Harpoon a Toyota' may seem a viable tactic, but most conservationist groups find blanket boycotts extremely difficult to initiate and oversee, and even more difficult to call off once begun. Furthermore, they do not particularly wish to penalize industries just because they happen to be Japanese.

The most potentially effective boycott so far proposed is probably that of the tuna industry. The Washington-based environmental consortium Monitor has pointed out that over one-third of all tuna on American supermarket shelves is Japanese in origin.

The advntage of the proposed tuna boycott is that the Big Three Japanese tuna producers are also the Big Three whaling companies: Taiyo, Nippon Suisan and Kyokuyo. The logic of this boycott, then, is that those who profit most from whaling will at least profit a little less from tuna fishing.

6 POISONING THEIR OWN

Under the headline 'Japanese Whalers Put People's Rights First', a New York foreign correspondent in 1981 interviewed Kunio Yonezawa in Tokyo. Wearing one (or all three) of his hats as deputy director-general of the government fishing agency, counsellor to the Japanese Fishing Association and IWC commissioner, Yonezawa observed: 'For me the number one issue is the rights of people.'

Most environmentalists find such a statement cynical and irritating to an extreme degree, especially as it implies the opposite about environmentalists, most of whom are activists in a wide range of other issues that directly affect humans as well as whales. Moreover, environmentalists are particularly concerned about such issues as industrial poisoning. And here they point out that if the whaling industry is so concerned about people and people's rights, why does it – and the Japanese government – ignore research conducted in 1978 and 1979 by Masashi Taguchi of the Institute of Public Health in Tokyo and Kenji Yasuda and Satoru Kurosawa of the Department of Agricultural Chemistry at the University of Tokyo? Their studies of mercury contamination in whale meat were presented to the IWC in 1979, to no effect whatsoever.

In a nation that gave the world the term 'Minamata disease' because of the disgraceful scandal concerning the mercury poisoning of its citizens, and the even more disgraceful goon-squad cover-up tactics that followed, it is remarkable that on the grounds of public health alone the Japanese government has not banned the sale for human consumption of all *odontoceti*, or toothed whale meat.

In short, the Tokyo studies pointed out that because of widespread industrial pollution of the oceans most marine mammals have suffered a considerable degree of mercury ingestion. In general the highest levels, as many studies the world over have shown, are in seals and toothed whales and dolphins, because of their considerable lifespan and their high level in the food chain (mercury tends to concentrate at each higher level).

This danger does not apply to the *mysticeti*, or 'baleen' whales – fin, minke or Bryde's – because they feed on krill, a short-lived species low on the food chain. (Blue, grey and humpback are also baleen, but allegedly are no longer hunted because of near-extinction.)

The Taguchi-Yasuda-Kurosawa study showed that on average

both fresh and canned sperm whale meat had a mercury content in excess of six times the maximum allowable standard established by Japan's Ministry of Welfare and the World Health Organization. Some special cuts, such as sperm whale 'bacon', had ratings as high as *40 times* the permissible level. Their study also showed that the orca and pilot whale had mercury levels *39 and 65 times* the maximum allowable.

Nor, as it turned out, were these the only studies. Similar results had been revealed in examinations of sperm whale meat by the scientists Tomita and Nishimura in consecutive studies as early as 1973 and 1974. In 1977 results of tests on Australian pigs should have been of interest to the Japanese, because 10 per cent of their whale meat goes into animal feed. Pigs fed on only 1 per cent whale meat built up mercury levels that were *5 to 10 times* those allowable for human consumption.

In 1978, in a survey conducted by scientists Arima and Nagakura on dolphins, mercury levels were unacceptable. The highest rating was for the bottlenose dolphin, which had an incredible mercury content *130 times* the maximum level permitted. Although far lower than the bottlenose rating, a real cause for concern was the striped dolphin, the most commonly eaten species, which had a mean value *12 times* the maximum allowable level.

So much for 'the rights of people'.

The ability of the government to ignore all international pressure on whaling is one thing, but to ignore the public health of its own people demonstrates the fishing lobby's degree of power over the politicians. It is one of the most appalling aspects of the entire whaling lobby and its avowed concern for people, and enough to make anyone cynical.

This is not to say that whaling is without criticism within Japan, but the occasional voices are not very loud. Eiji Fujiwara, professor of animal behaviour at Tsukuba University, wrote in *Asashi Science Magazine* in October 1981 an article to back up his statement that commercial whaling should be discontinued entirely for some time. The *Asashi Journal* in May 1982 ran an article by 'Shizu' with a similar perspective stating clearly: 'The view in Japan that this anti-whaling pressure is a part of the western response to the trade issue, is superficial and misleading. The demand for a commercial whaling ban is based on a purely biological view, which is aimed at avoiding the total extinction of the whale.'

Whale, published in 1983 was written by Takeshi Hara, a journalist who attended the 1982 IWC. It is a Japanese book which presents detailed arguments against whaling. In 1984 the Japan Union of Nature Conservtion, a coalition of more than 100 citizens conservation groups, called for Japan to respect the IWC's decision to halt commercial whaling by 1986.

Most remarkable of all, for many years now the Japanese government's own environmental agency has openly advocated an end to whaling. As early as November 1981 it was reported that, in a cabinet meeting, Kujiraoka, secretary general of the Japanese Environmental Agency, said: 'It's about time to stop whaling from the standpoint of nature conservation.' The Japanese newspaper reporting the event observed that 'there is some chance that criticism of whaling will come out inside Japan.'

Possibly, but it got short shrift that day in cabinet. Not only was the concept of a ban dismissed as outrageous but, the same day, the cabinet voted to ignore both the IWC quota for North Pacific sperm whales and the ban on the cold harpoon – harpoons without explosive heads – for the Antarctic hunt.

Evidently Mr Fish was still firmly in control.

11

ENDGAME

1 SINKING THE *RAINBOW WARRIOR*

On 10 July 1985 I arrived at the Charing Cross Hotel in central London just ten minutes before the start of the 12 noon press conference. The meeting had been called by the British umbrella environmental organization Wildlife Link on behalf of a dozen major environmental groups. The star speaker was Sir Peter Scott who addressed the major issues of the annual IWC meeting to be held in Bournemouth in four days' time.

Japan, the USSR and Norway were not going to abide by the 1982 moratorium decision and were going to continue commercial whaling beyond the 1985–86 season. Wildlife groups had just learned that Iceland and Korea also intended to continue whaling, but rather than attempt outright defiance, they used a loophole in IWC rules, simply calling what was obviously a commercial operation 'whaling for scientific purposes' and unilaterally issuing themselves a 'scientific permit'.

Sir Peter Scott called these plans 'blatant subterfuge', a 'flagrant abuse' of the IWC's procedures. These acts amounted to 'international hooliganism'.

Greenpeace representative Michael Neilsen pointed out that as their flagship, the *Rainbow Warrior*, was now stationed in Auckland for its summer campaign for a nuclear-free Pacific, it was ideally placed for the 1985–86 Antarctic whaling season. 'We will be there to confront the Antarctic fleets if and when they set out for the whaling grounds . . . Greenpeace will go anywhere in the world necessary to protect whales being slaughtered in defiance of the ban.'

As Neilsen spoke, a Greenpeace crewman floated lifeless in the dark and flooded passageways of the *Rainbow Warrior*, and the ship hung by her mooring ropes from the Auckland dock, diesel oil seeping from her ruptured hull. For at exactly the moment I was entering the Charing Cross Hotel, on the other side of the world an explosion rocked Auckland harbour. In New Zealand it was ten minutes to midnight. Beneath the harbour lights, the 150-foot, 400-ton *Rainbow Warrior* lurched, then keeled to her side as the waters rushed into her engine room.

When the first explosion hit, most of the crew ran in the darkness for the upper deck. Davey Edwards, the British first engineer, hurried down to the engine room to find the engines already submerged. Captain Peter Wilcox gave orders to abandon ship, but the Dutch first mate Martini Gotje and the Greenpeace photographer Fernando Pereira had already gone back below, Gotje to check cabins for missing crew and Pereira to salvage what he could of the photography equipment.

Gotje was climbing back up the stairs, and Edwards was pulling the elderly relief cook, Margaret Mills, from her lower deck cabin, when suddenly there was a brilliant flash in the water beneath the *Warrior*. The ship jolted violently as the second explosion punched a truck-sized hole in her steel hull, and the thunderclap of the blast awoke half of Auckland. Gotje leapt for the upper deck and Edwards and Mills fled with all their speed and strength as the seas raced down the corridors with them. As they climbed the stairs so did the water. With seconds to spare the trio – Mills still in her soaking pyjamas – reached the upper deck and scrambled on to the wharf with the others.

It was all over. Four minutes after the first explosion, twelve crew members were ashore and the *Rainbow Warrior*, completely flooded, had keeled over. She rested only partly above water because she was hanging by her moorings.

It would be another two hours before navy divers would be able to penetrate the wreck deeply enough to recover the body of the thirteenth crew member, Fernando Pereira. The Greenpeace photographer was 33 years old and left behind a wife and two young children.

Within a few days it was apparent that it was not whaling

interests that had sunk the *Warrior*, but rather pro-nuclear agents who wished to prevent the Greenpeace flagship from leading a flotilla to Mururoa Island to protest against continued French nuclear testing in the Pacific.

The Greenpeace conflict with France over Mururoa had been running for as long as the entire Whale War. In 1972 and 1973 Greenpeace's international director, David McTaggert, sailed a protest yacht into the test area. The first year he was rammed by a French military ship and then seized, and the second year he was savagely beaten by French commandos and then seized. However, the actions had been instrumental in bringing atmospheric nuclear testing in Mururoa to an end, though underground tests continued. After numerous nuclear accidents contaminated Mururoa, several other protest voyages were made, culminating in the 1985 Greenpeace initiative.

Fortunately for Greenpeace, the New Zealand government was firmly behind the Greenpeace effort to end nuclear testing in the Pacific. Prime Minister David Lange issued a statement that the government was treating the action as a high-priority terrorist act resulting in homicide.

Investigations revealed that the 44 lbs of explosives that blew up the *Warrior* had been planted by commandos from France's secret service, the DGSE Action Service. The scandal that arose in the wake of the arrest of two of the seven agents involved, Major Alain Mafart and Captain Dominique Prieur, was soon called France's 'Underwatergate'. After a series of government denials, it finally emerged that the operation was organized and massively financed from very high up in the military; consequently, both the chief of the DGSE, Admiral Pierre Lacoste, and Minister of Defence, Charles Hernu, resigned. In New Zealand, before the year was out, the two captive agents pleaded guilty to the charge of manslaughter (reduced from murder) and arson and were each sentenced to ten years in prison. However, in a shameful exercise of trade sanctions, diplomatic intrigue and economic blackmail, France forced reluctant New Zealand to release the agents within a year of their conviction and place them within the 'custody' of the French authorities where they might serve out their prison term in a manner deemed appropriate.

The sinking of the *Rainbow Warrior* and the murder of Fernando Pereira, although not brought about by the whaling issue, nonetheless resulted in a temporary advantage for the whalers. To be sure, none of the whaling nations were sad to see the *Rainbow Warrior* stopped at last.

2 IN THE BUNKER

ECO Editorial
1985 IWC Conference
Bournemouth

Three years ago in Brighton, as the votes rolled in on that extraordinary night, the world's conservationist community got a lift the like of which it has seldom seen. The International Commission, bowing to years of pressure and invaded by new members with the gall to insist that they had the right to sit on the commission along with the whalers, had finally forced the wishes of humanity on the last of the whalers: commercial whaling would stop. Period.

But this year in Bournemouth the victory of 1982 seems to be turning to dust. Through two-way deals, bogus scientific permits, and outright defiance of the commission, a handful of whaling nations threaten to continue chasing the whales to the ends of the earth.

Four days after the destruction of the *Rainbow Warrior* and the murder of Fernando Pereira, the IWC met in the Moat House Hotel in Bournemouth. Not only was the commission moated by the tightest security of any IWC meeting ever held but in an act surely symbolic of the entrenched whalers' position, the general assembly meetings were held in an underground conference room indistinguishable from a military bunker.

The 1985 meeting should have been a time of celebration for the conservationist forces, for this was the year the IWC was to begin the commercial moratorium by instituting zero quotas for all commercial whaling. The IWC did so, but the zero quotas for 1986 made no difference to the number of whales that would be killed. The sinking of the *Rainbow Warrior* more or less coincided with the end of the IWC as a body which exercised any control or restraint over its members. One way or another all whaling nations contemptuously ignored its zero quota ruling. Russia, Japan and Norway set their own quotas, and Iceland and Korea said they would kill under scientific permits.

There was, however, one good piece of news at the 1985 IWC meeting. This was that the hardline Russian commissioner had declared that the USSR would definitely stop whaling in 1987. This unexpected turn took everyone by surprise. The Russians refused to acknowledge any but unspecified 'technical reasons' for the shutting down of their fleet, though it is likely that the Russian fleet has had little capital investment for some years, for it is in a noticeable state of disrepair. The only reason the Russian industry has survived at all in recent years has been the ready and inflated Japanese whale meat market which has supplied much-needed foreign currency. However, the expensive prospect of refurbishing the fleet and the unacknowledged (but obviously considerable) effect of America cutting Russian fish catch quotas within US-controlled waters under the Packwood-Magnusson Amendment have negated any financial advantage that might be queried by continuing the industry. It is likely in the current economic climate, that the upkeep of the fleet is just too expensive and that by 1987 it will be scrapped, leaving Japan with the last pelagic whaling fleet in the world.

3 COURTROOM GAMBIT

Japan had for years used the IWC as a defence against the United Nations' call for a moratorium; when in 1982 the IWC also called for an end to whaling by 1986, Japan switched tack again, saying it 'saw no legal or moral obligation to accept any decision of the commission on such a proposed moratorium.'

This defiance would not have been possible in the face of the drastic sanctions of the Packwood-Magnusson Amendment, but the American administration once more betrayed its avowedly conservationist stand. Independent of the IWC, in December 1984 the Reagan administration, in defiance of its own legislation, came out of secret meetings with the Japanese. A two-way deal would allow the Japanese to continue commercial whaling (even of protected sperm whales) until 1988. Clearly, the Reagan administration was using the whales as a bargaining chip for its trade negotiations with Japan and to ensure further support for its own non-commercial Eskimo hunt.

However, no one involved really believes the Japanese have any intention of ending whaling in 1988. On 5 April 1985 the

Japanese Minister of Fisheries, Moriyoshi Sato, assured his people that the government 'will do its utmost to find out ways to maintain the nation's whaling in the form of research or other forms'. Everyone who has negotiated with the Japanese knows exactly what they will do when 1988 rolls around. They will continue as before and simply state that they have ended 'commercial whaling' and have entered a new era of whaling for 'scientific research'. This principle, firmly established by Iceland and Korea, will allow Japan to require a 'scientific' kill of whatever it needs to keep the industry going until 1990, when the commercial whaling moratorium will be up for review. At that time it will push for a resumption of whaling. The push will most likely fail, but it will give Japan another opportunity to reassert its 'objection' to the moratorium, and unilaterally 'resume' commercial whaling – resumption of the whaling industry that in fact never stopped at all, and that it would willingly continue down to the last whale.

By 1984, it was clear that the real battleground for the survival of the whales had been taken out of the forum of the IWC and put in the hands of the US courts. Twelve conservationist organizations represented *pro bono* by William D. Rogers and Jim Beat of the Washington firm Arnold & Porter immediately took the US State and Federal Departments to court for their failure to put the Packwood-Magnusson sanctions into effect and ban Japanese fishing within America's 200-mile limit.

In November 1984 the environmentalists won their case against the government in the Washington District court. However, implementation of sanctions was delayed nearly a year by an appeal. The appeal was heard, and in August 1985 the environmentalists won their second clear-cut court decision. The court of appeals ruled that the administration was required by law to implement sanctions, and must now do so. However, in a cynical miscarriage of justice, the government conspired to win even if it lost. By appealing to the Supreme Court, it once again delayed the sanctions, its strategy being that a final court decision could be delayed for another year, during which whaling would continue. Then, even if the court decided against the government, with a little guile the government could take a year to implement the moratorium amendment, which would bring it to the 1987–88 date it had promised the Japanese. Furthermore, if sanctions were delayed, there might quite likely be no action for the US to take. By 1988, because of new joint-venture fishing regulations, the Packwood-Magnusson Amendment may have no real power in law.

By July 1986 much of this legal manœuvring was purely academic speculation. The Reagan administration exerted extreme pressure on the Supreme Court, with the result that by a narrow 5–4 decision it reversed the two previous court rulings. The administration and the Japanese whalers had their victory, and the Packwood-Magnusson Amendment, in both spirit and letter, was destroyed as an effective legislated sanction against Japanese whalers. Most conservationists viewed the whole exercise as a vicious abuse of legal power and government money misused to betray a cause the American public has strongly supported.

4 STALEMATE

It was a time of crisis once again. The moratorium had failed. Japan – with the aid of the Reagan administration – destroyed it. In the eleventh hour of the Whale War, American negotiators snatched defeat from the jaws of victory.

If the administration had sanctioned Japan – as the American people had wished it to do and American legislation required it to do – Japan's and all other whaling operations would have ceased, and the Whale War would have ended.

But the administration betrayed the Save the Whale movement. Its refusal to use its sanctions to end the war opened the floodgates. Following Japan's lead, Norway filed its 'objection' and continued the hunt. Iceland and Korea shamefully exploited the IWC's loophole clause which allowed them to continue under the pretence of 'scientific research'.

Without even bothering to worry about the legality of doing so, and seeing the US impossibly compromised, the Philippines announced its intention to continue whaling. Elsewhere new pirate ventures were believed to be in the offing, and former whaling nations were, with Japanese encouragement, considering the possibilities for revived operations.

In a perverse way, one might be persuaded that the whalers had achieved something of an advantage in 1982 when the IWC had voted for a moratorium on commercial whaling by 1985–86. The resulting confusion to the public, the waiting to see if the whalers would abide by the decision, the long court cases – all of these dissipated the conservationists' energies and actions. While meeting after meeting, lawsuit after lawsuit, negotiation after negotiation went on, the whaling nations enjoyed four more uninterrupted years of business as usual.

By 1985 the only effective and highly visible direct action campaign in the Whale War was, in fact, launched against the Faroe Islands. This was a campaign to save the migrating herds of small North Sea pilot whales, which the Faroe Islanders had been slaughtering in thousands. It was a small-scale traditional hunt turned large-scale 'blood sport', according to the campaign initiators, the British-based Environmental Investigation Agency, an organization set up that year by Greenpeace-UK's founder Allan Thornton.

Although the Faroes campaign dealt with one of the lesser species of whales, which was not really in the main forum of IWC concerns, it was the one campaign that brought to public awareness the issues of whaling during 1985 and 1986.

All was not disaster, of course. The accomplishments of the conservationists in the Whale War have been extraordinary. The majority of the world's surviving whale populations are now protected. The number of whaling nations has been drastically reduced.

But unless loophole 'scientific whaling' is stopped and the moratorium enforced, the ground gained will be rolled back, and commercial whaling will not stop until the last whales are gone.

Since the UN vote in 1972, *every* international body and treaty that has any bearing whatever on whales has ruled that commercial whaling *must* stop. *All* are ignored by the whalers because no one will enforce such rulings. Japanese trading muscle is currently one of the most powerful economic forces in the world; few politicians have the nerve or will to resist it in a dispute over a few whales. (And the Japanese fixers were once again hard at work in the IWC: the conservationist-minded commissioners from St Lucia, St Vincent and Trinidad were notified just days before the 1986 IWC that they had been relieved of their posts. Each one was to be replaced by a commissioner thought to be more sympathetic to Japanese interests.)

By 1986 it appeared as if all means through law and negotiation, to enforce anti-whaling rulings had been nearly exhausted. Frustratingly, the whalers seem quite happy to launch into a new set of negotiations which they would gladly stretch out for another fifteen years – or to the last whale, whichever comes first.

Most believe that, at whatever cost, the Save the Whale movement must launch one last offensive before the IWC moratorium comes up for review in 1990.

5 RAGNAROK

They were driving in the dark when the police car pulled in front of them and deliberately blocked their way. Their hearts nearly stopped. The 20-year-old Californian Rodney Coronado and the 22-year-old Englishman David Howard were headed in the pre-dawn hours towards Iceland's Keflavik Airport just outside Reykjavik. In an hour they were scheduled to catch a 7 a.m. Icelandic Air flight to Luxembourg. When the policeman approached their car, both men felt certain they were not going to make their flight to Luxembourg that morning.

Coronado and Howard had good reason to be worried. They were agents of the direct-action Canadian-based *Sea Shepherd* conservation society. They had arrived in Iceland on 15 October 1986. Their mission was to inflict as much damage as possible on the Icelandic whaling industry. Their only other directives were that in so doing they must not use explosives, and they must not cause injury or loss of life.

On Saturday 8 November, after extensive undercover investigations, they were ready to act. In a hired car, that evening the pair drove through a blinding snowstorm out to Hvalfjordur, 45 miles north of Reykjavik. Hvalfjordur (meaning 'whale fjord') was the site of Iceland's only whale processing plant. The two activists knew that the isolated station would be deserted at a weekend. At 8 p.m. they arrived at the Hvalur whaling station and, in the excellent cover the snowstorm provided, broke into the station's main building and began their hard night's work. In the station's blacksmith shop they found all the equipment they needed. As Magnus Olafsson, the foreman of the station, was later to recount: 'they used sledgehammers to destroy everything in sight.' For five hours Coronado and Howard carried out their heavy demolition work: they destroyed all six of the plant's diesel generator engines; they wrecked all butchering equipment, machinery and refrigeration equipment. The pair then broke into six smaller buildings, and smashed the factory's extensive computers, VHF radios and control equipment, as well as files and records, and poured cyanic acid over them for good measure.

Shortly before 1 a.m. the saboteurs climbed into their car and drove rapidly back to Reykjavik harbour, home of Iceland's fleet of four whaling ships. Coronado and Howard knew that one of the ships had a night watchman aboard, while another was in dry dock. At 5 a.m. they made their move. Not wishing to allow for the possibility of human injury, they kept clear of the manned ship, instead quietly boarding the *Hvalur 6* and then the *Hvalur 7*. Having had considerable shipboard experience through overhauling and maintaining the *Sea Shepherd II*'s engines, the men knew exactly what they must do. They went down into the engine rooms of each ship in turn. There they patiently loosened the 16 heavy bolts on each ship's sea cocks, pried the valves open and allowed the sea to rush in.

By 5.40 a.m. the saboteurs had completed their work, dumped their tools in the harbour, and were back in their car driving out of Reykjavik. They had a plane to catch.

By 6 a.m. that Sunday morning the two 430-ton whalers were settling soundly on the bottom of Reykjavik harbour in 50 feet of water. It was at this moment that Coronado and Howard were pulled over by the police. The fact was that, just minutes before, their shipboard sabotage had been discovered and the police were immediately alerted. The ships had sunk rather faster than expected. Both men knew full well that early discovery was the major risk in their carefully timed operation, but they felt they had to take the chance.

As Coronado was the driver, he answered the usual police questions and showed his licence and identification. He stated their intended destination. He was then asked to get in the back seat of the police car while radio checks were carried out. Coronado must have looked somewhat suspicious on this cold morning covered as he was with grease stains and jeans soaking wet from the thigh down; however, from the line of questioning it soon became apparent that the police had asked him to get into their car simply so they could check his breath for alcohol. Coronado was extremely high on adrenalin at that moment, but he had not drunk any alcohol, so there was no problem proving sobriety. Coronado was then politely told they could continue on their way.

Luck was with these two young men, for although the sabotage had been discovered, through what was later labelled an error in judgment the police radio operators did not broadcast the incident as a general alert. Consequently, police patrol units such as the one that stopped the saboteurs had no knowledge of the incident. In fact, it was several hours before a general alert was raised, so even though their 7 a.m. flight was delayed for over half an hour, Coronado and Howard were well on their way to Luxembourg before the police began to piece the case together. It was a clean getaway.

Almost immediately after his agents were off Icelandic soil and known to be safe, Paul Watson announced from Canada that it was the Sea Shepherd organization that had committed the actions. He made it clear that he was responsible for and had directed his agents to do what they could to cripple the Icelandic operation. He said: 'We wanted to cost the whaling industry in Iceland at least two years' profit. We are convinced we did.' The attack *was* costly. Icelandic officials estimated the damage conservatively at something in excess of US $2 million.

Watson himself did not participate in the raid, only because he felt he was too well known to remain unnoticed. If Watson had wished to gain the attention of the Icelandic people, he certainly achieved that aim. Prime Minister Steingrimur Hermannsson called an emergency cabinet meeting and followed it up with a special debate in the Althing (Iceland's parliament) on the Monday after the attack. That evening, Hermannsson addressed the nation on both radio and television, with a speech full of sound and fury.

'The saboteurs are regarded by the Icelandic government as terrorists and all efforts will be made to get the people who are responsible prosecuted for this inhuman act.'

Attorney-General Hallvardur Einarsson stated that the government would attempt through all possible channels to have these saboteurs extradited, then prosecuted in Iceland.

Paul Watson replied that he would frankly welcome criminal proceedings and attempts at extradition. They would give him an international platform to present the case against what he saw as Iceland's illegal whaling operation.

In retrospect, Iceland was probably the most obvious target for activists in 1986. It has been a highly visible hard-line whaling nation since those initial encounters with the *Rainbow Warrior* in 1978 and 1979, when it fired five harpoons over the protesters' heads and twice seized their ship. There had been, in fact, a plan in 1979 by another radical environmental element to sink the Icelandic fleet. However, Portuguese and Spanish pirate ships were considered a higher priority at that time.

The last straw for the activists was Iceland's initiation after the moratorium of the strategy of 'scientific' whaling. Under self-issued permits, Iceland planned to kill some 800 fin, minke and sei whales over a four-year period. As before, the Icelandic whalers will continue to make tens of millions of dollars by selling this 'well-researched' whale meat to the Japanese. The Koreans immediately saw the advantages of this system and adopted it, while the Norwegians and even the Faroese have visited Iceland to take instructions on how they too can profitably 'research' whales.

One may well ask how this system of 'scientific' whaling differs from commercial whaling? The simple answer is: it does not. Most members of the IWC Scientific Committee have concluded that the unasked-for 'research' would be of little or no value considering that decades of whaling research at very high commercial levels has yet to be analysed. Some benign research which does not involve killing the animal might be useful, but somehow this approach does not greatly appeal to the whaling nations.

Many conservationists were outraged that Iceland would dare argue a new-found love of research into whaling. Sir Peter Scott of the World Wildlife Fund called it 'international hooliganism' disguised as science. Fearful that population studies would show serious depletion, Iceland has for decades failed to supply to the IWC even minimal research statistics on whale populations. (From 1974 to 1980, for instance, it was required to mark 200 whales a year for population studies. Iceland's whalers found it too bothersome to mark more than 10 a year.)

Iceland achieved its catch quota through the notorious IWC commissioners' horse-trading sessions, which are closed to observers and press.

The new stance taken by Iceland is that of responsible scientists providing statistics needed and desired by the IWC. Many of the IWC Scientific Committee are frankly disgusted with the project. As one IWC scientist openly stated in 1986: 'As a scientist, I suppose I should hope for the miracle of enlightenment at Hvalfjordur – but, like most of my colleagues, I also hope never to be connected in the public mind with the charade being enacted there.'

Paul Watson warns that the Icelandic action is a signal for a final confrontation between whalers and activists. Norway, Korea or Japan may be next. In Watson's eyes, they are all pirates now. Other groups and individuals are at work, in a less physical but equally determined manner.

Many in the IWC have asked why conservationists are determined to end *all* commercial whaling, wondering why there is no room for flexibility. They feel that a carefully controlled, sustained harvest of whales is perfectly possible. This argument has held the UN ban on whaling at bay since 1972 and has resulted in the slaughter of hundreds of thousands of whales. Today eight of the ten great whale species are rare enough to be considered commercially extinct. (The eight species are: right, bowhead, grey, blue, humpback, fin, sei and Bryde's whales.) It is probable that some whale populations have already dropped to the point of no return, and even without further hunting, they are on the road to extinction. The grey whale is the only species known to have recovered from intensive whaling. After decades of protected status blue, bowhead and humpback whales have not noticeably rallied. The once common right whale has not been hunted for a century, but has never made a comeback.

Perhaps a voice from within the IWC's Scientific Committee might make the point. In 1985 Dr Sidney Holt wrote:

Commercial whaling has never been, is not now, and economically speaking probably never can be, based on sustainable exploitation from a stock which is kept near to or above its biologically optimal level. Whaling is essentially an extractive industry, akin to mining. Targeted depletion of one whale 'seam' stops when it becomes uneconomic to extract more, and the industry moves on to other places and species.

Until none remain.

An end to the Whale War will come, one way or the other. It is a clear choice: do we extinguish the industry, or do we allow the industry to continue on its way and extinguish both itself and the last of the whales together? It is a climax right out of Icelandic mythology, the apocalypse known as *Ragnarok*, that fatal last battle between the gods and the giants that ends in extinction for both.

PART FIVE

And God created whales. *Genesis 1: 21*

12

THE VALUE OF LIFE

1 TREASURE HUNT

There is something enchanted about a long beach and a bright sea the morning after a big storm. The sky clears, the sun emerges, and clean fresh air sweeps the shore. In common with most children who grew up next to the sea, I saw the aftermath of a storm as a time for beachcombing, a time when the possibility of finding some lost treasure presented itself.

One such morning, as I walked the intermittent shingle and sand shoreline near my home, the sunlight was brilliant and everything on the wet shore seemed illuminated with an unreal light. The air was salty and sharply cool, filled with the smell of washed-up kelp heaped in huge tangles like so many monstrous legendary kraken dashed on the beach. There was half a wrecked rowing boat, the beams and a piece of roof from someone's beach house that had been destroyed by high waves in the night. There were some large, damaged shipping crates, and on one of the sandy stretches I found a couple of agates glistening in the sunlight like big jewels as the water lapped over them.

What I was really looking for were glass fishing floats. There were a few plastic ones with pieces of net attached, yet I wanted the big glass balls – I thought of them as fortune-tellers' crystals – usually deep green. Many of my friends had green crystals, and I had found one myself and given it to a schoolfriend. But what I really searched for was a crimson crystal. We believed they were from the Japanese fleet, and only one schoolfriend had one of these. This was real treasure. Perhaps, I thought, I would find one this day.

I was investigating some washed-up crates that lay against several big drift logs where the waves slapped listlessly after the exhaustion of the storm, when I saw something half-floating on the shingle shoreline. It was about twice the size of a baseball and weighed no less than a couple of pounds. It was unevenly shaped, rather oblong. A curious lump, it was marbled grey and whitish, was rather waxy in texture, but did not give way easily to a poke with my finger. I could not really determine whether it was organic or something man-made. There didn't seem to be any strong discernible scent to it, so I suspected it must be a melted lump of some sort of man-made plastic or perhaps sun-melted wax.

It was a mild curiosity, and I could not see much use in it. If I took it home and it turned out to be organic, it would probably end up being buried deep in the back garden. So I simply chucked it back into the sea and watched it bob off on the tide before I continued my search for treasure.

It was more than twenty years later that I learned with a shock of recognition what that mysterious, rather ugly lump on the shore was. It was ambergris. The legendary 'grey amber' of the sea that in a time before the last few decades of synthetic perfume fixatives was worth more than its weight in gold. At the time I found it, that piece was still worth many hundreds of dollars. So much for my early years as a treasure hunter.

I tell this story because it says something of how we value things. I regarded with disdain the grey amber worth more money than I would make until I reached adulthood, and went off in search of a few pennies' worth of blown glass. Where is real treasure to be found? Something is one moment worthless and without meaning to us, and the next – in another context – of the highest value.

Ambergris is a perfect example. Like the pearl is to the oyster, it was rarity found in only a very, very few. Ambergris was also something of a mystery. It was the most valuable product of the sperm whale, although not until the eighteenth century, when 20 pounds of it was found in a whale, was its source known. Until then it was only found – as I had found it – washed up on the shore. The reward could be phenomenal. One whale in 1915 was said to contain $60,000 worth of the substance in its intestines. But such finds are extremely rare. We may be wiser than we once were, but we still have no idea why and how ambergris forms within whales, why only the sperm whale produces it, and why only one among thousands has been found with it in its body.

Once, the sperm whale was hunted primarily for the strange and very fine spermaceti oil from a huge reservoir in its head, and for the oil distilled from its blubber. It was clear that oil was what was valuable. Even the big blue whales, until the last few decades, were simply flensed of the blubber for oil, and the meat, bone and all other parts were dumped. The Antarctic island whale stations, with their oil-rendering works, had hundreds of thousands of tons of peeled whales discarded in the shallows about them.

Today, that once discarded meat is the primary product. The pirate whalers who hunt down the whale to get the highest prices kill a whale, cut from it only its prime dark meat fillets, then dump the whale, blubber and all, back into the sea.

Treasure hunters are strange beings. What is valuable to them is arbitrary and constantly changing. The value of ambergris dropped when chemical fixatives for perfumes proved as effective and far cheaper. The price and need for spermaceti oil fell when the jojoba plant was found to produce an oil with exactly the required characteristics. In the last few years, when the import ban on the sale of whale products came into effect in the United States, one of the immediate results in former whaling towns such as Nantucket was the soaring price of whale ivory that was already in the country. Sperm whale teeth that previously were hardly worth a dollar each suddenly sold for $200 or more; the tusks of sea unicorns – the narwhals – were being auctioned off in New York at prices more appropriate to the horns of real unicorns.

Still, only very recently have people found that the huge animal itself, alive and free, might have some intrinsic worth beyond its market value in oil, meat, ivory or ambergris.

2 THE CACHALOT

Beyond the mystery of ambergris is the mystery of the sperm whale that produces it. Beyond barrels of oil and tons of meat, what we *don't* know of the sperm whale, or cachalot, this most continuously hunted and familiar of all whales is quite staggering.

For instance, take one of the most basic aspects: how does a sperm whale feed itself? We know, of course, that it eats largely squid – even the deep sea giant squid of fables – and whalers have found sharks, barracuda, skates, rays and albacore in its belly. The peculiar thing is that all of these creatures, particularly the speeding albacore and the quick darting squid, can either outrace or outmanœuvre the big sperm whale that, on a good day, might reach 10 miles per hour on a short run.

One of the most fascinating answers – speculations – comes from contemplating another question. What is spermaceti oil for? In the sperm whale's head is a huge cavity filled with this extremely fine oil which, until recently, was used as transmission oil in Rolls Royces and earlier was used for the smokeless spermaceti candles. It is a yellow oil which hardens in the air into a whitish wax. The cavity, called the case, in a bull whale is about 5 feet deep and 12 feet long, and contains up to ten barrels of oil. It is generally accepted that in part the case serves as an echo-location and communication system. Most cetaceans have some such cavity. Dolphins have a fatty area called a melon, which is believed to serve the same purpose. However, in the sperm whale the size is so vast that some other purpose is thought to be involved.

Soviet scientist V. A. Kozak in 1974 introduced a 'third eye' concept that makes the whale sound like it has its own indoor motion picture theatre. This theory suggests that the spermaceti organ works as a 'video-acoustic system' which transfers sound energy into images, using the rear wall of the case as an 'acoustic retina'. More interesting, however, and bringing us back to the riddle of how the whale feeds itself, is the Flash Gordon-style 'stun-ray gun' theory. Two other Soviets, V. M. Bel'Kovich and A. V. Yabalkov, in 1963 proposed that the spermaceti organ is used to focus a shock wave, a kind of projected sonic boom, to stun its prey. It was 'an effective instrument for stunning and immobilizing prey far away'. Too space-age? Not according to the Israeli study of A. A. Berzin, who in 1972 supported the Russian conclusions and wrote: 'When mobile squid and fish are discovered, the ultrasonic beam narrows and focuses on them, its frequency sharply increases, and the prey is stunned and seized.'

More recent dolphin research at the University of California at

Santa Cruz by Ken Norris and Ken Martin in 1985 tends to support this stun-ray theory. Also, recordings have been made of sperm whales using what is believed to be this high-intensity, low-frequency blast of sound. The blasts are intense rather than loud, and to the human ear sound like rifle shots fired over the clicking echo-location sounds that are used to scan for victims. Tests indicate that fish or squid subjected to the full force of the blasts would not just be stunned but would have parts of their body tissue destroyed, and would quite likely be killed. (Music, no doubt, to the American military. Let no one be surprised if the Pentagon is already at work on some sort of underwater star wars laser system.)

These are only the beginnings of our exploration of the mysteries of the cachalot, and but a glimpse of the treasures it might reveal to the science of men. The biggest mystery of all, of course, is the mystery of its huge brain. How and why and to what purpose has the sperm whale's brain evolved to be the largest and most complex brain ever to come into existence? Again, we can only begin to speculate. The trick is, we must allow the animal to survive long enough at least to resolve such riddles if we are to increase our knowledge of communication and non-human intelligence. Which again brings us to the question of value.

3 SCRIMSHAW

Scrimshaw is carved and engraved whale ivory. A traditional craft of increasing rarity, the whalers of the Azores have found it newly profitable as tourists buy up their handiwork at once unheard-of prices. Many of the tourists are Americans, and although it is illegal for them to import whale ivory into the US they usually succeed in smuggling it through with their luggage. Scrimshaw is usually made from the teeth of the cachalot, and so, in the Azores, the teeth are at present the real treasure. These go to the crews of the boats, and over 50 per cent of their income from each whale derives from the sale of the teeth. The Azore hunters take about 130 protected sperm whales a year. Nearly all the products of the whale are exported.

The Azore whalers use traditional whaling techniques. Their whaling vessels are 35-foot, narrow, double-ended, sailing–rowing canoas and motorized support launches which tow both canoas and the caught sperm whales. At present there are less than 10 canoas and 13 support launches actively whaling in the Azores.

One motor launch tows a canoa out to the whales, and another launch follows them to attend later to the sperm whale. (Sometimes the launches are also used to herd the whale and exhaust it, and even at times for lancing, powering along beside the whale and stabbing down at it.) Each canoa has a removable sail and six oars, so that it can quietly approach the whale without alarming it. There are seven men to each canoa including the master and the harpooner.

The environmentalists' main objection to traditional whaling is that it causes such a slow death. Humane societies are unhappy with even the exploding harpoon gun methods, which generally take 20 minutes or more to kill a whale. Traditional hunters claim an average time of one hour and 20 minutes to make a kill. After the whale is harpooned, it is slowly tired by the playing in and out of the harpoon line. Death usually comes when the exhausted, wounded whale is lanced with a long, thin, unbarbed spear.

Some hunters earn a small supplementary income by making the whale killings a spectator sport. For a fee, they will take tourists out on the launches to watch the slaughter.

Those tourists who buy scrimshaw might pause to consider not just the price if they are caught smuggling the whale ivory back through customs but also the price of the acquisition of the ivory in the first place. They might read the following eyewitness account of a whale hunt. This particular hunt, recorded by ecologist David Moody, took place in July 1979; similar hunts continue today.

The whale had been harpooned at 10.15 in the morning. The first observation was logged at 12.15 when the whale, a bull sperm of nearly 50 feet, surfaced near the canoa, with the launch in fast pursuit, the harpooner on the bow throwing a lance just as the whale sounded. Apparently the master already realized that they had an unusually wary and resourceful whale on their harpoon. Normally these whalers harpoon, chase, lance and kill their whales in about an hour and 20 minutes. Already this whale had succeeded in avoiding the fatal lancing from the canoa for two hours, so the master had elected to use the motor launch, which is ordinarily not employed for lancing.

12.18 – Whale surfaced, launch pursues, lance thrown.

12.35 – Lance thrown twice from canoa, the harpooner having been taken back aboard the canoa.

12.36 – Another lance thrown, the whale sounds, no flukes shown.

12.42 – The canoa signals the launches to come near, with extra line ready to pass the canoa. The whale has run out 2,700 feet of line in a deep dive. The master keeps tension on the line, letting it pay out in spurts.

12.50 – Launch is standing by with extra tub of line rove ready.

13.05 – Waiting, the whale has been down half an hour now.

13.08 – The whale surfaces 150 yards away from the canoa. The canoa signals for the launch as the whalers bring in the line hand over hand.

13.12 – After about 20 spouts the whale sounds, flukes high, the canoa being towed slowly behind.

And so the hunt goes, hour upon hour, the brave bull whale, through the day lanced again and again, dives and eludes, dragging the whalers after him. Never once does he attempt to attack his hunters. An impossible *ten hours* later, the light is fading and the launch driver is for cutting the line and letting the whale loose, but the master, who is known for his tenacity, determines to hold the whale through the night.

20.40 – Surfaces and sounds at the approach of the launch. Through the night the whalers worked the harpoon line, trying always to keep tension on it – paying out when the whale sounded, hauling it in hand-over-hand when he surfaced. The launches followed their same tactics, harrying the whale, forcing it to dive as quickly as possible, and always trying to herd it back towards the island. The master and harpooner got no sleep, the other oarsmen got an hour or two over their oars. It is two days after the full moon, the night lit by its soft, hazy presence, but no lancing is attempted during the night. The sea is very calm.

The hunt begins again at dawn.

06.25 – Surfaces near us for a few spouts, and sounds as the launch nears. A light breeze from the southeast has rippled the sea surface. The whale continues his canny tactic of circling underwater and surfacing as far away from the launch as possible, usually on the other side of the canoa and in the opposite direction of the harpoon line.

06.55 – Surfaces, spouting every 10 to 13 seconds. The harpooner goes into the canoa, and the canoa creeps up behind the whale, slowly, hand over hand. The canoa rows the last 50 yards. The whale is swimming very slowly. The harpooner throws the lance repeatedly, in the end using the lance to jab deeply without throwing. Twenty-one thrusts are made, and the whale begins spouting fountains of blood, though some are clear.

07.05 – Sounds slowly, grievously wounded.

07.20 – Surfaces and swims slowly in a wide circle, the launch herding.

07.25 – Sounds, flukes askew, resurfaces immediately.

07.26 – Sounds, flukes up, resurfaces after a minute, spouting every 13 seconds. Blood, swimming in a circle. The canoa hand lines itself in slowly, passes the whale still taking in the line, the whale continuing its slow circle on the surface. The canoa turns for a final closing, the harpooner ready, the whale sluggish, but he sounds when the lance is thrown, resurfacing immediately at left 90-degrees angle.

07.35 – Sounds as a dolphin pod comes by leaping and cavorting.

07.42 – Surfaces, dolphins have circled and return. The whale is spouting every 10 to 13 seconds, some spouts are almost clear, others seem almost pure blood fountains.

07.46 – Sounds. The dolphins swim off at high speed, leaping in low eight-foot arcs. The whale surfaces, seems tired, confused, hurt. The harpooner thrusts his lance 18 times more, the canoa stays close.

08.00 – Still lancing.

08.07 – Still lancing, there is no point in counting. The harpooner is working close enough to jab the lance deeply, over and over.

08.17 – Still lancing, whale spouting every 16 seconds, heavy blood, he is lying still in the water, just able to maintain his equilibrium.

08.20 – Thirty seconds between spouts, heavy blood.

08.28 – Occasional spout is clear of blood, the whale is wallowing but upright.

08.41 – Twenty seconds between spouts, whale upright,

canoa waits nearby for the death which must come soon.

09.00 – Heavy spout of blood, the whale rolls slightly, tail showing.

09.12 – Having great difficulty staying upright, the canoa and the launches wait, an occasional spout is still free of blood.

09.15 – Shows right flipper in a dizzy slow motion roll, one fluke emerges.

09.36 – Tail showing constantly, the whale lying partially on his side.

09.40 – Canoa moves in.

09.55 – The whale is dead.

The whale has taken 23 hours and 40 minutes to die.
This is the price of scrimshaw.

13

THE REVOLUTION

The concern for the future of whales is a positive sign of spiritual
awakening and the birth of eco-consciousness. . . . We are entering a
new age of earth-mind and earth-minding.

DR MICHAEL FOX
Ethics of Whaling Symposium, 1980

1 THE VISION

Imagine the universe as we all once imagined it.

By night a great dome of black velvet studded with the bright
diamonds of the stars, and the crescent moon like a white ship
sailing over its wide expanse. By day the sky illuminated by the
fiery chariot of the sun, the dome paling to an azure blue.

Beneath the dome is the earth – a vast, flat platter with all the
big heaped land masses, mountains, forests, valleys, lakes,
islands; all enclosed by an encircling sea.

And beneath the earth is a great fish – very like a whale. It
bears up all the world, and the firmament as well, upon its broad
back. Safely through the infinite abyss, the dark oceans of chaos,
the whale-fish makes its way.

It is one of those fairy-tale visions we made up and told
ourselves in the childhood of the human race to explain how life
was sustained in the evident chaos of the universe that we feared
might swallow us up at any time. Today we are amused by the

vision, we tell ourselves we know much more of the world and the universe.

However, knowledge is not the same as wisdom. Life on earth is ancient, and man and his science are still very young. By comparison, the whales are an ancient tribe. For 30 times as long as humanity has existed at all, the whales have been the largest-brained, most intelligent beings on this planet. Carl Sagan, in his *Dragons of Eden*, wrote: 'The brain of a mature sperm whale is almost 9,000 grams, six and a half times that of the average man. . . . What does the whale do with so massive a brain? Are there thoughts, insights, arts, sciences and legends of the sperm whale?'

The writing and experiments of Dr John Lilly and others have brought about widespread speculation of the possibility of an alien intelligence that is at the very least our equal. (In fact, Lilly advocates, in the realm of pure intelligence, whales are our superiors.) Some argue that this is the domain of science; others believe it is a kind of spiritual quest. But whatever the case, it is increasingly obvious that the argument must be for the survival of whales, not just for their sake but for our own sake as well – whether we see that in terms of science, or knowledge, or spirit, or imagination, or more complex arguments of ecological balance.

Despite the sophistication and advancement of science and technology, in certain respects we have lost a degree of true wisdom. In a deeply intuitive way, perhaps we 'understood' in that onc all-embracing fairy-tale vision how all creation depended on balance and harmony with nature. An old lesson we must learn anew.

2 THE CONCRETE WHALE

While many a Save the Whale demonstration congregates around an inflatable whale, one grass-roots Save the Whale organization finds it necessary to travel to its extremely stationary, land-loving whale. This is a much-heavier-than-air whale that would find it as difficult to swim, or even float, as a real whale would to fly.

This whale is called Conny, and it is a life-size, 40-foot ferro-concrete sperm whale which sits in a park outside the Children's

Museum of Hartford, Connecticut. It is the symbol of the rock-solid support the Save the Whale movement has in what in the previous century was America's premier whaling state, the state of Herman Melville and the Nantucket archetypal whaler Captain Ahab.

Conny was built by the Connecticut Cetacean Society and is an example of how a small group of concerned individuals can motivate an entire community and direct it into ecological concerns. Begun in 1973 by its charmingly obsessed and eccentric executive director Dr Robbins Barstow, as a local support group for Project Jonah, by 1975 the Connecticut Cetacean Society managed to have the sperm whale designated Connecticut's official state animal, and the following year the society built Conny. It was a diabolically clever tactic. State representatives found that as a matter of loyalty, a peripheral issue had overnight become a central issue. It was difficult for any state representative not to have an uncompromisingly conservationist stance on the threatened extinction of the official state animal. The slaughter of the state animal of Connecticut by foreign nations – *especially* the Russians – was greeted with outrage. As well, schoolchildren would learn of the state animal and how it and all the great whales are now endangered. The citizens of Connecticut should know what could be done for whales, how whale sanctuaries could be advocated, and how support could be given to the anti-whaling movement.

When the Indian Commissioner to the IWC in 1981 declared that he was entirely fed up with debates that viewed the whale as some kind of 'giant meatball', he was viewed by the Japanese and Russian contingents as some kind of lunatic let loose in their midst. Such attitudes were, the Japanese declared, irresponsible, frivolous and had no place in a serious forum such as the IWC, where a responsible attitude towards whales as a resource must be taken. However, as most environmentalists were keen to point out, the Japanese attitude was that 'responsible' use of the whale was simply a euphemism for controlled slaughter, and it was not the only way to view whale resources.

Far from being frivolous, the non-consumptive utilization of whales through tourism, film work, recordings and education was already a $300 million industry by 1981. Nearly ten years earlier, in 1972 (the year of the UN commercial cessation declaration), the Mexican government recognized that there was a far greater potential for making money out of live whales than from dead ones. In that year the coastal lagoons of Baja became the world's first whale sanctuary. These are the mating and. calving grounds where the California grey whales end their 7,000 mile migration – the longest of any mammal – on North America's Pacific coast. Here the spectacular leaping mating rituals are carried out, and observation towers were built and tour boats organized for a vast and growing tourist potential. It has become one of the great natural wonders of the world which has been lucratively and harmlessly exploited.

The Save the Whale movement has, since 1972, resulted in the establishment of many other sanctuaries and areas where whaling is forbidden in national waters. The result has been for some species to return to coastal waters they had not been sighted in for a century or more. The famous leaping and singing humpback whales in sanctuaries in Hawaii and Australia have proved terrific tourist draws, as have the migrating grey whales off California and the orca killer whales in the Northwest Pacific. Whale watching tour businesses have sprung up all along the Atlantic coast of North America; in Newfoundland, the Gulf of St Lawrence, the Bay of Fundy and New England. One tour boat operator from Provincetown, Massachusetts, on his own takes some 18,000 whale watchers a year out to Cape Cod Bay to sight whales.

In 1983 Robbins Barstow, who launched Conny the concrete whale, originated another rock-solid, heavyweight concept: the Whales Alive global conferences on the non-consumptive utilization of whales. This was a kind of anti-IWC that Barstow originated with the help of many other Save the Whale groups, especially that of Maxine McCloskey's California-based Whale Center, Christine Stevens's Animal Welfare Institute, the World Wildlife Fund, the International Union for the Conservation of Nature and the government of the Seychelles, which hosted the 1983 conference. Whales Alive took up the cause of benign research, tourism, film, recordings, books, the science of whales in the ecosystem, and educational value.

The important thing about such events as the Whales Alive conferences is that they demonstrate that the Save the Whale movement is not simply negative; that it is not really an *anti-*

whaling movement but is essentially a *pro-whale* movement; that the potential for the non-consumptive use of whales is a far more productive industry than the killing of whales under its present short-term, rapacious conditions. Perhaps Whales Alive or something like it will eventually become the real forum for the management of whales, and the IWC will pass into extinction. Whales Alive is the forum of life; the IWC – as presently constituted – is the forum of death.

3 MIND IN THE WATERS

Many people now perceive a mystical aspect to the whales: animals that have survived 20 or 30 times longer on this planet than man and possess a brain that in some cases is six times bigger than the human brain. The focus of Project Jonah, for instance, has always been on this aspect. Project Jonah produced a book entitled *Mind in the Waters* which concentrated on the mental powers of whales and dolphins and the possibility of communication with these species. Indeed, it has proven to be the one aspect that most intrigues people, for its seems to evoke a kind of nostalgia for a mythical utopian age before the biblical Fall, when men and animals lived as one. It is perhaps this strange vision of a return to Eden that motivates many to communicate with cetaceans.

The nature of whale and dolphin communications only became widely known during the Second World War, when Allied navy engineers were using underwater listening devices to spot submarines. Their headphones were flooded with whole concerts of bizarre chattering, clicking, burbling, clunking, rattling and creaking. These were the voices of whales and dolphins. Later came the complex but definitely musical sounds of the humpback whale, and the impossibly powerful low-frequency trans-ocean sounds of the fin and blue whales that cetologist Ron Storro-Patterson of the Whale Center described more like 'sensing an earthquake' than hearing.

In 1946 researcher Arthur McBride in Florida discovered that one purpose of all this noise was that dolphins and all toothed whales 'echo-locate' – that is, use underwater sound like a radar system. This enabled dolphins, for instance, to catch fish and avoid nets even in the dark. Later research revealed that the clicking sound in dolphins originated in a soft tissue area in the forehead called the melon, and the signals were received in the lower jaw which acted like an antenna. Among the many mysteries of this process is the question of how these sounds are produced. Whales and dolphins have no vocal chords, and there is no evident muscle or bone that is mechanically capable of making such sounds.

All this was of interest to only a small part of the population until Dr John Lilly published his book *Man and Dolphin* in 1961. It was Lilly who brought to the public's attention the concept of interspecies communication with dolphins and whales. In the mid-1950s, it was discovered that a dolphin would 'communicate' with humans like any other trained animal, swimming to the surface and whistling and making strange sounds through its blow-hole. By 1957 dolphins were also mimicking human speech. By 1961 Lilly stunned many of his colleagues by advocating the idea that cetaceans were not just like very smart dogs, but rather 'these cetacea with huge brains are *more* intelligent than any man or woman'. Many scientists reacted as if it were their duty to defend the pride of the human race and attempted to discredit Lilly's work.

Others have chosen to work with larger cetaceans: Thomas Pulter of the Stanford Research Institute and director of its Biological Sonar Laboratory began for the first time to record orcas in a systematic way when Namu the killer whale, taken on Vancouver Island, was kept in the Public Aquarium in Seattle in 1965. He discovered conversations between whales seven miles away with the captive animal. He described a very complex exchange of sounds that could only be described as an animal language.

Others such as early Canadian Greenpeacer Paul Spong and Californian Jim Nollman have experimented with recorded music and live instruments fitted with underwater amplifiers as a means of attempting to communicate with the orcas of the Northwest Pacific.

However, as the naturalist Jacques Cousteau, who among his many films about whales made the beautiful *The Singing Whales* in 1975, has said of attempts to develop two-way communication between men and cetaceans: 'No sooner does man discover intelligence than he tries to involve it in his own stupidity.'

By this he meant the immediate interest in dolphins and whales

expressed by the military. Since 1965 both Americans and
Russians have been training dolphins for potential use in espionage
and sabotage work. Since 1968 orcas, belugas and pilot whales
have been used for similar missions, and quite commonly for the
recovery of lost torpedoes and missiles in deep water. The nastiest
use of cetaceans by the military so far seems to be the case of the
killer dolphins during the Vietnam war. Dolphins served as
underwater sentries around American ships anchored in the Bay
of Tonkin. They had large hypodermic needles strapped to their
beaks and were taught to search out any human swimming in
the water and to prod him with the needle. The needle was
connected to a high pressure carbon dioxide cylinder. The result
was a massive injection of the gas into the lungs or stomach, and
the swimmer literally exploded like a burst balloon.

Dr Lilly and many other researchers have no desire to develop
cetaceans as tools of war. In fact, in 1967 Lilly released his
captive dolphins on the grounds that 'I no longer wanted to run a
concentration camp for my friends'. He continued to work with
complex computer analysis of dolphin language, an attempt at
code-breaking what he calls 'dolphinese'. His ultimate goal is a
machine that directly translates conversations between men and
dolphins.

Others are taking different approaches to interspecies communication. Some of the best results have been achieved by Dr
Louis Herman at the University of Hawaii, using a vocabulary of
visual and acoustic signals with captive dolphins. Dr Kenneth
Norris in Santa Cruz, California, is analysing recordings of wild
dolphins. None of them underestimates the difficulty of the
translation process. Dr Norris points out that dolphins and
whales see and taste through sound and possess many other
faculties of which we are now only vaguely aware. 'It is very
hard for us to imagine sensory systems and processes we do not
have. . . . It's a bit like a man from outer space tapping into the
Bell System centre and trying to make sense of all the beeps and
switching sounds.'

Difficult though it may prove, study of the large and complex
cetacean brain convinces most scientists of the animal's intelligence and capacity for dialogue. And it is here that many believe
humanity has its best bet for truly communicating with an 'alien
intelligence', not out in the stars hundreds of light years away,
but more obviously in the seas of our own world.

4 SONGS OF PEACE

In 1970 the largest single pressing of any phonographic record in history was made. Capitol Records, in co-operation with *National Geographic*, pressed 10 million copies. Remarkably, the recording artists who merited this mass publication were totally unknown to the public. More remarkably, the singers were not even human. Most astounding of all, it was a smash hit. The humpback whale had suddenly become the world's greatest recording artist.

The recordings of the 'Songs of the Humpback Whale' were made by the world's foremost whale musicologist, Dr Roger Payne. Dr Payne, like Dr John Lilly, is a neurophysiologist. He first studied owls at Cornell University and then became permanently sidetracked with studying whales. As he had also an extensive musical background, he was fascinated with the 'songs' of the whales. His studies were considered fairly abstract and esoteric when he began his work in the mid-1960s, backed by a variety of academic and ecological groups. Then, overnight, the 'Songs of the Humpback Whale' went from an obscure scientific recording to a multi-million best seller. The huge voices of these opera stars of the deep were going out to the people of the world.

The humpback whale is considered the most playful and most agile, as well as the greatest singer, of all the great whales. It takes its name not from any deformity but from its tendency to arch its back when it dives deep. When dragged up on land by whalers, the humpback appears awkwardly made, but in its element it is perfectly designed. It is capable of spectacular leaping, and when viewed under the water by divers it proves to be sinewy and agile, using its 14-foot pectoral flippers to steer and wing its way through the water. Hawaiian divers, finding the name inappropriate, call them the Great Winged Angels. (This is a mistranslation of their scientific name, *Megaptera novaeangliae*, literally 'Great Winged New Englander', not angel.) However, as the divers see it, the whales' distinguishing flippers make them appear like huge angels winging their way through the blue heaven of the sea – an image out of D. H. Lawrence's poem 'Whales Weep Not': 'the burning archangels under the sea keep passing, back and forth, / keep passing archangels of bliss'.

Why the Great Winged Angels sing is not really known but, as scientists and students of music, Roger Payne and his wife Katherine find themselves drawn further and further into the study of the eerie symphonies. 'The humpback is the only known animal species whose songs are continuously undergoing changes, changes that are complex, large-scale and rapid,' says Katherine Payne. 'The whales use a technique very much like one a good composer uses to create beautiful and interesting music. For example, Beethoven sets up rhythmic patterns and musical themes we all recognize and expect to recur. Then he surprises you with a variation. Every humpback whale song I've heard surprises me just the way Beethoven does.'

The whales sing songs in solo, in duets, trios, quartets and even entire schools in chorus. Whale songs are like human dialects. All whales in one place will sing one dialect, while their cousins in another breeding ground will sing a completely different arrangement.

Songs change and evolve over weeks and months. The changes affect the songs' lengths, timing and number of sounds. Dr Payne equates these with musical themes in symphonies, or, in a simpler analogy, songs with musical rounds which are dropped out, split apart and rearranged. After a time, gradually all phrasing is replaced and a completely new song emerges.

In the course of the conflict of the Whale War, there is evidence that a kind of revolution has taken place. More than all the ecology activists and their supporters, it has been the whales themselves who have been most responsible for this, by virtue of their impossible hugeness, their gentleness, their intelligence and the vocalizations that we now call whale songs. These are songs of a peace movement that extends beyond the conflict of man and man. It advocates peace with all life on earth.

We are hearing the music of other worlds within our own. It is cutting through the propaganda noise and the machinery of our own industry. Perhaps it will bring us away from the monomaniac view that all the world was created for our sole use. Perhaps it may help guide us towards a revolution in the human mind that will bring us back to the philosophy that sees that we are but one of the beings among many others who are meant to live harmoniously on this planet. That old vision: a return to Eden.

Dr Michael Fox, author and veterinarian, articulated the wider significance of the whale as indicator of a revolution of human consciousness, a new philosophy of man and his perspective of life on the planet. Speaking at the 1980 Ethics of Whaling Conference, he said:

> The concern for the future of whales is a positive sign of spiritual awakening and the birth of eco-consciousness. Let us not lose our faith, courage and commitment. The ethical, humane and ecological crises of today can be seen in a positive light as shaping forces in our own evolution and transformation. We are entering a new age of earth-mind and earth-minding. Our greatest challenge is to begin the awesome task of healing the earth and transforming human consciousness while there is still time. In the restoration of the earth we will realize our true human potentials and rejoice not in our own creations, but with all of creation in empathetic resonance and communion with the whale, the wolf and the eagle of whose essence is the significant 'otherness' of our being and becoming.

Today we find schoolchildren on landlocked farms in America or in German industrial cities who have never even seen the sea and yet know more of the mysterious whales than the world authorities did twenty years ago. Artists, authors and actors together with office workers, housewives and old-age pensioners give over their resources and time to creatures they only know through imagination. Many musicians like Paul Horn, Paul Winter and Judy Collins have recorded their music to whale accompaniment, while scores of others have used their own voices to raise funds for the whale campaign.

The world is changing because the human mind is changing. Common cruelties are no longer tolerated. Aristotle Onassis's whale penis barstools are no longer acceptable. Target shooting by navy and airforce personnel on whales twenty years ago was occasionally mentioned by the press as an amusing anecdote. When such an incident was reported in the 1980s, an American navy commander was rapidly court-martialled.

For me, one extraordinary event indicated how much human attitudes have shifted since the beginning of the Whale War in 1972. This was the mission in February 1985 of the Soviet icebreaker *Moskva*. The second-largest whaling nation in the world – which that very season was ruthlessly violating its IWC quotas and slaughtering whales in the Antarctic – was also the same nation whose icebreaker was fighting its way through the Bering Strait's Arctic pack ice into Senyavina Sound to *rescue* whales. Nearly a thousand beluga white whales had been entrapped when they had pursued a shoal of fish into the Sound and the ice had closed behind them. Although Soviet naturalists had kept the whales alive by helicopter food drops, they nevertheless were doomed to starvation had it not been for the determination of the *Moskva* which for weeks fought the pack ice to reach them.

It seems quite amazing that the rescue was made, for the cost was extraordinary. As one Soviet official said, referring to the cost of airlifting fish in to the whales and pushing the icebreaker through, 'They are already golden whales.'

But even more marvellous, in its way, was what happened when the *Moskva* crew broke through to the whales and attempted to draw them out. Through the ship's sound system they piped music over the icy waters to attract the whales' attention. Then, like the Pied Piper, music playing, the *Moskva* led its children out of the dangerous caves of ice that had threatened to entomb them forever.

EPILOGUE: WHALE SONG

'And enormous mother whales lie dreaming suckling their whale-tender young
and dreaming with strange whale eyes wide open in the waters of the beginning and the end.'

D. H. LAWRENCE, Whales Weep Not

Perhaps it is the whales that should have the last word. I sit and listen to a recording of the humpback whales singing their distant, otherworldly songs, their strange operatic sonar soundings sent out over immense distances. A whale singing alone, then two together, then in a massive choir in the wide universe of the world's oceans. I think of a speech given in 1980 by Dr Roger Payne, when he accepted for himself and his wife Katherine the Albert Schweitzer Medal, awarded annually by the Animal Welfare Institute for outstanding contributions to animal welfare.

The Paynes have studied whale song in the waters off Hawaii, Mexico, the North Pacific, Bermuda and Argentina. Like other scientists, they believe that some means of communication between whales and men might eventually be possible. And in the very least they know that by studying their songs they will enlarge the knowledge of communication and non-human intelligence. In certain ways they seem not unlike the scientists in the film *Close Encounters of the Third Kind*, looking for a musical alphabet to communicate with these alien beings – although, if anything, on this planet perhaps we are the aliens, not the whales.

In his speech, Dr Payne quoted that often cited statement by the wise and visionary nineteenth-century Indian chief, Seattle: 'What happens to beasts will happen to man. All things are connected. If the great beasts are gone men would surely die of a great loneliness of spirit.' And in his speech Dr Payne concerned himself with mankind in a world devoid of all 'the great beasts' and the prospect of humanity 'dying of a great loneliness of spirit'. This is, of course, a valid fear and concern, for year by year we can see that we are in fact pushing species after species towards extinction.

Listening to the recordings of whales singing their huge arias in the deep lonely sea, I imagine for a moment that perhaps, just perhaps, it may be quite different. Not less terrible, but different. If our present mad quest for domination and power leads to the obliteration of our species in some terrible conflagration of nuclear war, it is likely that most of the animals of the land and air will be consumed as well. When such dark thoughts come to me, I have a small prayer: that we do not leave this an empty planet, that the seas will survive. And if one grand life form in those seas might survive us, let it be the whales.

Allow, if others are silenced, the songs of whales to rise up through the darkness to the distant stars. Let these be the guardians of the planet, great archangels of life in the wide seas below. Then, perhaps, it will be them and not us who will lament, sadly aware, in that great brain, that something is gone out of the tumultuous terrestrial world, knowing, no doubt, in ways we cannot know, wise in ways we are not wise.

Then, in a planet empty of life save in those 'waters of the beginning and the end', there will be a long, long time of waiting. Eventually, once again, it will be safe for life to creep out upon the land. And perhaps, as life emerges on the shore, in the sea foam the whales will sing again. Huge lullabying midwives to a new world.

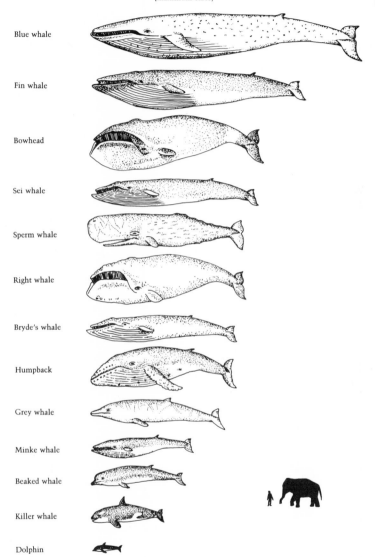

Scale chart of the major whale species
(maximum sizes)

Blue whale

Fin whale

Bowhead

Sei whale

Sperm whale

Right whale

Bryde's whale

Humpback

Grey whale

Minke whale

Beaked whale

Killer whale

Dolphin

161

INDEX